SMALL
CURES

A POEM BY
Della Hicks-Wilson

Andrews McMeel
PUBLISHING®

SMALL CURES

Andrews McMeel Publishing
a division of Andrews McMeel Universal
1130 Walnut Street, Kansas City, Missouri 64106

www.andrewsmcmeel.com

21 22 23 24 25 BVG 10 9 8 7 6 5 4 3 2 1

ISBN: 978-1-5248-6996-0

Library of Congress Control Number: 2021933773

Editor: Hannah Dussold
Designer: Tiffany Meairs
Production Editors: Jasmine Lim
Production Manager: Carol Coe

ATTENTION: SCHOOLS AND BUSINESSES

Andrews McMeel books are available at quantity discounts with bulk
purchase for educational, business, or sales promotional use.
For information, please e-mail the Andrews McMeel Publishing
Special Sales Department: specialsales@amuniversal.com.

for
the unhealed

and mum,
my first healer.

everybody told her, "don't worry
there is more love in the sea."

she fished for days,
only to catch herself.

CONTENTS

Preface ix

I. DIAGNOSIS I

II. TREATMENT 61

III. RECOVERY 101

PREFACE

∞

In May 2013, I posted my first poem on Tumblr, completely unaware that this would be the beginning of the book you are holding today. Perhaps it's true that you don't choose the book you've always wanted to write; the book chooses you. And then, slowly, the work begins.

My blog was a strange private-public journal of sorts; many poems, usually short, written straight into the "new text" pop-up box with minimal to no editing. When I had to review and select pieces for this collection, I had more verses than I ever remembered writing, publishing, or even feeling; hundreds. Some mere fragments, others full thoughts, memories, or parts of what seemed like imaginary dialogue made up of soothing reminders, warm directives or candid observations; some technical, some not. But almost all of them linked by one common theme, love, or more specifically, the desire to love better.

I knew from the outset of curating this collection that I wanted to weave these laconic verses together into a book-length poem that told a cohesive and progressive story. However, it was also important to me that I was faithful to the original texts by not changing them too much, or at all, solely to fit this purpose. I wanted the initial emotion or idea that compelled me to write the poem in the first instance to be honored, whether I fully remembered it or not. The book is then, in part, a montage or collage of textual memory. Some of the work, though, has never been published.

Writing this book has been a long and creatively challenging journey, and I am thrilled that through it all—the years, the uncertainty, the changes—my words have finally found their way home to you in a volume and form I am deeply proud of. So, without any further ado, here she is. Welcome.

—Della Hicks-Wilson

SMALL CURES

I. DIAGNOSIS

the first cardiologist
i ever saw
explained to me
that unfortunately,

someone can only possibly love you
as much as their heart
knows how to love.

∞

the problem is, she sighed—

we cleanse
our bodies
but not our hearts
enough.

∞

and so,

sometimes there is so much pain in both,
loving and leaving
feel the same.

∞

but she said,
honey, don't worry—

there are some of us
who are born
with holes in our hearts.

there are others
who have theirs
carved out much later.

∞

every ache
has its own purpose.

∞

and,

everything has a heart.
even the moon.

sometimes, most times,
it's not the whole of you that dies.
but parts.
and only you attend the funeral.

the people we once loved.
the ones who said it back.

eventually you'll learn
how to live
with your ghosts.

everything we try to forget,
our blood remembers.

i cannot tell you where to put your pain.
i can only tell you
that this pain is not your main destination.

it is. and it is:
one point on a map
of a thousand others.

a place you have come to.
a place you will leave.
for you are only
traveling through hurt,

and sometimes
it all looks the same
because hurt
has many stops.

but darling, i promise
you are aching to arrive somewhere
so much better.

remember,
you were light first.
the body came
way after.

∞

and darling,

broken or not,
our bodies
are our only vessels.
in this life,
we choose
what we will carry.

∞

so, i didn't tell her
how often i think—

maybe if we would have had the same wounds
we could have healed each other.

the moon waited for me.
why couldn't you?

loving you is easy.
loving you is muscle memory.

i loved. and i loved.
until all that was left
was bone.

∞

someone once told me—

once love is made,
it exists someplace.
even without the lovers.

∞

it's not just ghosts
that come back.
the living do
too.

with you,
i always felt like the ocean.
whole and vast and yours
when you said,
i am the only thing
you have ever loved.

secretly, i was convinced
i would be the only body of water
to never see a wave.

so when you gathered
all the empty shells you'd laid
and surely left,

well—that's when i knew:
something outside of you
shouldn't be able to make you feel
so big.

∞

i miss you in places i didn't even know existed.

come back.
come back.
return
whatever peace of me
you took.

∞

she said—

honey,
do not let your beautiful mind become a battlefield.
just because someone has shown you their weapons
does not mean you have to accept the war.

∞

on the last day of love,
give yourself permission
to remember the first.

darling,
your soil is too rich
to let words that aren't
deeply rooted in your truth
soak in.

∞

all words,
like us,
are ninety percent water

you can choose
to drown
in the ones that hurt

or,
you can choose
to let them
cleanse you.

∞

last night,
when i was wandering through
the deep, thick forests of your eyes,
you asked me what i was thinking

and surprised, i quickly painted you
a picture-perfect lie
about how your eyes remind me
of the color of bark.

actually, i was wondering
if branches on trees
ever get tired of reaching,

and if they do,
then so can i.

∞

like skin
or fears
or dreams,
little by little,
we can shed
what we love.
not everything
or everyone
can keep growing
with us.

sometimes we love the wrong people,
and that's okay.

you shouldn't have to
break your self
and move your pieces.
if they were designed for you,
they would fit.

remember,
the heart is not symmetrical,
and neither is love
or the stars.

but take it,
and align what you do.
align what you do
with what you long to un-feel.
every. time.

in the grand scheme of love,
it's true, that you, yes you
may become a small,
map-less country:

indistinct,
landlocked,
unchartered.

but darling,
don't ever be afraid
to take permanent ink,
and draw your boundaries.

in fact,
outline your entire body
if you have to.

honey, you haven't got time to break him open
to see if he has love inside there. leave him—
just like that—and see if he shows it.

you deserve a love
without footnotes,
asterisks, or question marks.

∞

tell me you won't make your soul a cemetery
for all the things that could have been.

i wish somebody had told me
that loving someone,
knowing how to love someone,
and someone loving you back
are three entirely different things.

sometimes,
loving yourself will mean
un-loving someone else.

we aren't born with hurt
rattling inside our bones.
no.
we learn to hurt
in the ways hurt people
teach us to.

∞

she said,

darling,
you feel heavy
because you are
too full of truth.

open your mouth more.
let the truth exist
somewhere other than
inside your body.

honey,
there is no shame in ending a war.

∞

and i said yes,
but—

every mourning
without you
is like a new death.

the truest poems
are not written,
they are felt.
words remind us.

i think i
breathed you
too deeply,

my lungs
couldn't
forget you.

∞

on those
nights
when your
heart
is hungry,
i wonder
if you
remember
how i
once
broke
my self
in two.
just
to give
half
to you.

they say
that the body repairs itself at night when we but sleep.
i've always wondered, though,
when do we repair our souls?

i am covered in the memories of you.

i wish i knew
how to love
in pencil.

the years
do not pass.
they just find
places to live,
quietly, inside us.

∞

she reminds me—

you are too full,
too alive,
to be pining after
half-empty ghosts
to come back

or,
to love you.

eventually the day will come
when i will take these chapters,
each named after you

and place them
somewhere far
on the tallest shelf
in the very back of my head.

i have already begun
collecting the dust
i will conceal your name with.

nothing.
no, nothing,
should make you
pluck the stars
from your sky.

we are small suns.
each day lighting
or blinding
our own paths.

i am done
mourning
the living.

∞

the most painful of heartbreaks
is missing somebody
who doesn't exist.

∞

it took you years
to write his name
on every inch
of your softest walls

so,
it may take you
just as many
to un-carve him from them.

there is blood,
but also stars
in your bones.

you'll break.
you'll bleed.
you'll shine.

there has to be a bottom to this sadness.

there has to be a bottom to this sadness

because even the bluest sky

        stops falling.

∞

and one day,
this sadness
will become a song
you just know some
of the words to.

on one side,
there is loss.

on the other,
a revolution.

∞

darling,
survival isn't something you do.
survival is what your heart is made of.

II. TREATMENT

day one

if your appetite seems to have left with them,
or you find yourself in a strange kitchen
with an insatiable appetite for all the wrong things,
remember, to never let that heart of yours go hungry.
darling, feed your heart
at least three portions of poems a day.
poems with pulses louder than the voices
telling her it will not be okay.

it will be okay.

day two

in spite of what you might think,
people have never been pills
or long-term cures,

and swallowing them now
bit by bit or even whole
will not make you more alive
or any better.

so when the nights get rough,
do not reach for a body
like a bottle in the darkness.
they were not made
to save you.

day three

learn from the moon
that darkness
is just an invitation
for you to create
your own light.

day four

when we are healing,
our clocks should be set differently.
in fact, our clocks should not be set at all.
and time should only exist in two measures:
what was then.
and what is now.

day five

healing will not always tell you
when she is on her way,
what she will look like,
or how long she will stay,
but like the moon,
she is always coming.

so darling, pull your curtains back,
keep your windows wide open
and every room inside of you unlocked,
healing is coming.

day six

remember this:
your heart is both
your softest place
and your strongest muscle.
it breaks. and beats.
at the same time.

day seven

when you lose a habit,
which became a function,
which became love—
the body will want to replace it.
or put it back in place
almost immediately.
but you take your time.
you let your body know
it can survive without it.

day eight

sit with your pain.
hold its hand.
it is as scared
as you are.

day nine

cry.
put the fire out.
darling, you are still burning.

∞

day ten

whenever you feel
the thickness of guilt
forming in your mouth,
swallow it.
as quickly and as hard as you can.
for the body knows best
how to break it down
into forgiveness.

day eleven

despite all that she's been through,
the earth keeps on spinning

and like mother like daughter,
so do you.

day twelve

honey, everything.
every. thing.
is happening as it should be.

day thirteen

try to retrace your steps.
go back to the places
where you gave
too much of yourself.
mark them all.
never go back again.

day fourteen

you may both share the same name
and occasionally look in the mirror
and see one another at the same time.
but darling, do not confuse
who you were
with who you are.

day fifteen

the scariest thing about healing
is blowing up buildings.
watching the giant walls
fall slowly. you know hurt.
you've lived inside her so long
that you don't know anything
about being the architect
of your own home.
now, from above the wreckage,
this is the time to learn.

day sixteen

there are towers of hurt
inside all of us.
each hurt
piled on top of the other

some days,
threatening to fall.
some days,
falling.

but you

                    survived,

and now,
here you are,
standing on top
of your tower of hurts.

look down.
look down.
see how far you have come.

∞

day seventeen

pain doesn't wilt,
it blooms in silence.
speak it
back into the earth.

day eighteen

before you ever let regret
spend the night—or two—
know that you will not
be able to bury him in the morning.

truth is,
regret is one of the only things
that lives longer than we do.

day nineteen

darling,
even in the riptide of anger,
stay in love.

love drowns anger
every. time.

∞

day twenty

after your lungs take a breath,
you do it.
your lungs breathing
and you taking a breath
are not the same thing.

day twenty-one

the world can
do its best,
and blow
and blow
and blow

but
your fire
is fierce
and lit
inside you.

day twenty-two

forgive them
for what they could not give you.

now,
give it to yourself.

∞

day twenty-three

i hope you learn the soft way
that holding on
to what must go,
or what has gone
won't make a hero
out of you.
it's letting go that requires
the most strength.

do it,
and i promise
you'll draw from muscles
you never knew you had.

day twenty-four

and now
that your hands
are not filled
with another body,
feel yours
for the knots.
then untie
every lie
they ever told you
about you
from you.
darling, please
take your time.
unpick them
as slowly
as they
un
picked
you.

∞

day twenty-five

when your heart
is thirsty:

do not settle
for rainfall.

wait
for the flood.

∞

day twenty-six

honey,
be still. be patient.
peace is always busy
working her way back to you.

day twenty-seven

do you think that the night
ever questions whether the day
will come and swallow her darkness?

do not doubt for a second,
a beginning is coming.
a beginning is coming
to eat all your endings whole.

day twenty-eight

when your loved ones come
armed with plows,
ready and willing to help you
nurture your heartland,
open the door.
let them.
for you can only grow alone
and harvest yourself so much.

day twenty-nine

darling, you mustn't forget
the heart breaks once, twice
maybe a few times in a whole life.
but one hundred thousand times a day,
your heart pounds,
your heart stays.

day thirty

each morning
ask your heart
how it would like
to be loved

and each day,
do that.

day thirty-one

only water what comes back.
you cannot force dead flowers to grow.

thankfully,
your smiles
will always be seeds.

plant them,
indiscriminately
and everywhere.

day thirty-two

twice before sunrise, soak
in deep, deep love with yourself.
stay, long enough to cleanse the wounds
beneath the wounds you cannot see.
they are the ones that need it the most.

day thirty-three

write
until you're not sure
whether the poems are healing you
or you are healing the poems.

∞

day thirty-four

be thankful.
love has beaten you
tender,
as it was supposed to.

day thirty-five

a list of the things you know now:

better.
better.
better.

∞

day thirty-six

take words
and art
and love
and dreams.
and water yourself
daily.

day thirty-seven

honey, beware—there may be storms coming that shake your branches until you don't have a leaf left. but never, never, let them pull you from the roots.

day thirty-eight

tend to the relationship you have with yourself.
first.
last.
always.

∞

III. RECOVERY

years after the fire,
i read somewhere
that trees spend their lives
building walls around
their wounds so
they never spread.
and i couldn't help
but think how different
our roots would be
if people did that.

nobody ever tells you
that saving yourself,
usually, always from yourself
is the whole story.

we spend our beginnings
and middles
desperately trying
to rewrite the end.

honey,
be kinder to your story.
you are the first
and only draft.

Della Hicks-Wilson

with every apology,
there is a language we learn.

∞

sometimes our scars say things
we will never understand.

and so—

Della Hicks-Wilson

i will say to my daughter
and her daughter,
"see your beauty
without a compliment
or a mirror."

who taught you
that the value
of a woman
is the ratio
of her waist
to her hips?
or the circumference
of her buttocks
to the volume
of her lips?
your math is
dangerously wrong.
her value
is nothing less
than infinite.

∞

let's not tell our girls that the most precious thing they own
is a flower between their legs. something they can lose.
something that can be plucked. instead, let's tell them
that they are sacred gardens. and every flower they grow
in their lifetime matters. and if they should lie under bodies
they one day regret, they should never feel like crushed petals,
too damaged to be healed or to be loved. no one has died.
there is no such thing as a body count. tell them: the most
precious thing about you, has always been you.

our bodies
like land,
crave water
and understanding.

∞

emptiness means
there are places in you
you are not done fully loving.

∞

honey, remember that we are more fiber than flesh.
we fray.

we don't lose ourselves.
we unravel,
slowly.

pay close attention.

travel yourself first.
the world,
later.

∞

there are too many of us accepting lovers who say:
"i partially love you."

when you leave,
a new voice
takes your place.

i spend the night whispering
sweet somethings
into my own ear.

it's true,
there was a time
when a call from you
would make me spring
into full bloom.
your voice would
offer me petals,
and i would scatter
my roots onto the base
of your drums, secretly
hoping to sow seeds
of forget-me-nots.
but please
do not think
that you were,
or ever will be,
my sun.

imagine:
i was a whole
country of love
before you
discovered me.

before you
"discovered me,"
imagine:
i was already full,
i was already found.

∞

they say—

be careful of what you let
into your heart.
it
may never leave.

∞

but,

i survived every one of your goodbyes.

when i am still
and think,
of all the little miracles
happening inside of me—
i
can barely
breathe.

∞

honey, who said that the love of your life
had to be a man or a woman
you haven't even met yet?
maybe, you are destined to be
the greatest love of your own life.

you could spend your whole life
waiting for the moon to moan your name.
but nobody, nobody can yearn for you
like you.

no, darling.
yo(u) complete you.

∞

Della Hicks-Wilson

fill yourself
with yourself.

∞

when love arrives
it should never say,
am i the only love here?

remember,
you are sacred land.
choose your travelers
wisely.

∞

loving yourself is magical,
but it is not magic.
it is an unremarkable,
necessary decision.

∞

you can't pour yourself into someone else
and wait for their love to refill you.

listen to the waters.
they will always warn you when
the river you have been left
gasping from,
leads nowhere.

∞

Della Hicks-Wilson

honoring your breath first
is the beginning of everything
and the end of everything else.

you can't make them stay.
and no.
you didn't make them leave.

Della Hicks-Wilson

you are more than more than enough.

and maybe you gave him
more love
than his heart could hold.

Della Hicks-Wilson

honey, what you crying for?
didn't you know?
didn't somebody tell you,
a deep remarkable love
should scar you?

when your heart breaks,
the next time you'll love
either twice as hard
or only with one half.

your soul
doesn't have bones
for a reason.

∞

find someone
who speaks
to the quietest
parts of you.
and doesn't say
a word.

Della Hicks-Wilson

if everyone understood your beauty
it wouldn't be nearly as magic.

poems are trapdoors
to our secret selves.

Della Hicks-Wilson

we bury our dreams
in open graves
and wonder why
they haunt us.

stop asking if you are capable of being loved,
as if being loved had a prerequisite.

how many refuges must you run from
before you realize that you
are the safest place you can go?

you
can never leave
you.

∞

you should have been your first love.

it is counterintuitive to think
that whatever causes a wound
can be the same thing which heals it.
so why do we believe this is possible in love?
why do we think that our breaker
can be our fixer?

for years,
we tried
breathing under water.

we tried
and tried
until the air gave up.

∞

she said—

darling,
did you forget
that we age
like the sun—
backwards?

every tomorrow
we burn brighter
than our past.

do not allow
hard memories
to turn your
softness to stone.
be clay,
simply coming back
to the earth
for a while.
for a while,
remember them
as gently
as you can.

you have scars
from the wars
that came,

but also,
from the wars
that left.

Della Hicks-Wilson

the sun
does not race
the moon.
each
has its time.
each
has its place.
like we do.

fall back
into your
own arms
and stay.
stay.

maybe
this is the way
we forgive
ourselves.

if tomorrow these wings should fail me,
or i should fail these wings,
it is comforting to know
that somewhere, out there
waiting,
are newer, wiser
versions of me.

∞

honey, see i told you.
everything will be okay in the morning,
and every morning after that.
yes, every morning after that
will break. and heal. like we do.

and honey, you make sure you love yourself
just as recklessly as they left you.

there are so many
other souls.
and yet,
we humans,
all ego, all dust,
obsess over the ones
that were never made
for us.

there are endings,
and there are beginnings,
and the two always meet.

∞

breathe yourself in.
and love yourself out.

∞

Della Hicks-Wilson

breathe yourself in.
and love yourself out.

breathe yourself in.
and love yourself out.

∞

Della Hicks-Wilson

there is no cure
for that.

Della Hicks-Wilson is a British poet and writer of Caribbean descent from London, best known for her short viral poems and spoken word videos, which have garnered over a million likes and shares to date. Her bestselling debut collection *Small Cures* was originally self-published in 2020 and selected by *Stylist* magazine as a Best Summer Read of 2020. She holds a BA and MA in English from the University of Cambridge, close to where she resides.

Zemmour & Gaullism

Marlon Ettinger

Ebb Books
Unit 241
266 Banbury Road
Oxford, OX2 7DL

Paperback ISBN: 9781739985257
Ebook ISBN: 9781739985264

British Library Cataloguing-in-Publication Data
A catalogue record for this book is available from the British library.

Typeset in Garamond
ebb-books.com

For An

Contents

Zemmour at Trocadéro — *3*

"An Algerian Berber Jew" — *20*

Zemmour Today — *23*

From Resistance to Government — *33*

The PCF Today — *44*

Gaullism — *49*

De Gaulle and Algeria — *53*

Zemmour's Foreign Policy — *64*

The Officers' Letter — *68*

The Fight for the Countryside — *72*

A Civil War on the Right — *78*

A Pack of Hypocrites — *85*

The Great Replacement — *87*

Endnotes — *94*

Zemmour at Trocadéro

"We don't feel safe," Dominick told me. She had come from Cote d'Azur – a 12-hour bus ride to Paris' Place du Trocadéro – to see Éric Zemmour speak.

Jean, a retired teacher from Cote d'Azur, tried to put it in terms an American like myself could understand. He compared Zemmour to Donald Trump. "We're trying to escape *la Gauche wokisme*," he said.

If you believe Zemmour's campaign, he was one of around 100,000 people who came to the Trocadéro in the West of Paris on March 27th, 2022. Some media outlets estimated around 15,000. Before the day, Zemmour's campaign predicted around 55,000 attendees. Jean proudly showed me his ticket which said he was the 52,298th person who'd registered for the event.

It was a boiling, near cloudless day – hotter than most people expected. By the end of the day just around 5:00 PM the crowd was filled with burnt faces.

"We didn't expect this much sunlight," Benjamin Couchy told the crowd. "But the sunlight at Trocadéro is you." A ubiquitous media presence early in the *Gilets Jaunes* movement from Toulouse, Couchy is now a spokesman for Zemmour's campaign.

I also talked with Antoine de Loissy, from Dijon, who ran a business involved in mustard production. He was very active politically and involved in the Parti Conservateur, a reactionary party within a party in the mainstream right-wing party Les Républicains (LR). De Loissy had voted for Éric Ciotti in the primary campaign for Les Républicains. Ciotti promised a hard line against immigration and ran sharply to the right. He made a stir in one of the primary debates when he called for a French Guantanomo Bay to be built to aid the fight against radical Islam. All of the Ciotti people, Antoine assured me, were for Zemmour. Ciotti himself, while supporting Valérie Pécresse now, promised publicly to vote for Zemmour in the second round if she was knocked out.

The right had split in 2017, Antoine explained to me, between the Fillon current of LR and the Alain Juppé current. Juppé, once Jacques Chirac's Prime Minister and until recently the longtime mayor of Bordeaux, was the more centrist man. He had chosen to support Macron, Antoine told me, while Fillon had mostly retired from political life.

"The Fillon current is carried more by Zemmour," Antoine said. Despite this, he knew for a fact, he said, that Fillon doesn't want to support Zemmour.

Laure had come from Dijon too.

"He's really the only one who can protect our values," she said. She had voted for a Le Pen for 18 years – first Jean-Marie Le Pen, then Marine.

What changed?

"Marine," she said.

She also complained about the rising cost of living. Though she had recently gotten a 500 euro a month raise, she said she was living half as good as she had been before.

Arlette, from Cote d'Azur, tried to get me into touch with her son Vincent, a police officer in Toulon. She wanted him to show me just how bad things were. She texted him, and he replied with information about how I could contact the precinct's comms department.

"There's a hierarchy," Arlette explained.

I talked with Christian, from Dijon. He said people who came to France needed to assimilate. "It's not a question of racism, it's a question of culture ... when in Rome do as the Romans do."

He also complained about the state of television. He said he hadn't watched it in the past two years.

"I can't support ... reality TV... MasterChef etc. It's too politically correct."

The good chefs should go forward, he explained, not those that are more "telegenic."

The last time, he pointed out, a couscous dish had won. He had no problem with couscous, he said – he liked couscous – but he believed the dish had just been passed through because of political correctness.

Christian had voted for Marine Le Pen in 2017, but "she's finished – she had her chance." The problem with her, Christian said, was that she was born into politics. Zemmour, as so many people told me proudly, wasn't a politician.

"Marine Le Pen," Christian finished pithily, "was more in opposition than in proposition."

His wife Laurence agreed. In 2017 she voted for Fillon in the first round, then Le Pen in the second. She taught physics in a middle school and said that education had been degraded. She said that every year students were passed to the next grade without having learned what they needed.

Echoing a line of Zemmour's, she claimed there were students in 6eme (11 to 12-year-olds) who didn't even know how to read. I asked her if she'd seen students who didn't know how to read herself.

"Of course!"

She also rejected parity, where equal numbers of men and women are required in official positions. By extension, she rejected feminism, which she said was synonymous with parity. "When they say Zemmour is sexist, misogynist, it's not true."

Witolel, from Toulon, owns a business fabricating sails for boats. "In France we're taxed and taxed and taxed," he complained. He was supporting Zemmour, he said, to "bring back the value of work." He said he couldn't afford to hire new employees because of the taxes he had to pay as a business owner. "We pay the salary of a person twice," he said, referring to taxes he had to pay for the employee and as the business owner. Not being able to hire more employees because of this, he said, meant he had to turn down work.

"Stop taxing us!"

He'd come overnight on a bus with his son Eloe, 20, who studies landscape design. Eloe was voting for Zemmour because of "insecurity," he said, a word which refers to the perception of an out-of-control France where crime is rising and ordinary people are under attack by criminals and antisocial elements.

Whereas Eloe's first introduction to Zemmour was during the campaign, Witolel had followed him on television for the past 10 years. He admitted, like a guilty secret, that he had an older son, 24, who was on the left.

Macron? Antoine asked sympathetically.

"Worse than that. Mélenchon."

Witolel's first name was Lithuanian. After I'd talked with him I heard him chatting with a couple from Dijon about how his family was from Poland. Somebody asked him if he spoke Polish. No, he said, getting passionate. "When you live in a country, you should speak its language." His grandmother had thought the same – she refused to teach his children Polish.

"You must not be part of Poland," said Witolel, "you must be part of France."

The stage framed the Eiffel Tower between the two wings of the Palais de Chaillot. The grand, sand colored "*moderne*" buildings, with blocky columns, flanked the deep blue stage. The roofs of each wing of the Palais were crawling with tiny security figures on top.

Before the speeches began there was rising, triumphant

music: a tinkling piano riding on a hum. Eventually an ethereal young female voice that seems to whisper the grandeur of France comes in. The music rises with anticipation. A low frequency bursting through the sound system rumbles your chest.

"The music is superb," Antoine tells me.

A who's who of the Zemmour campaign speaks: Stanislas Rigault, 22, Zemmour's very young campaign manager, comes out first; the crowd chants his name over and over again (after the event, Rigault takes selfies with the crowd swarming up to the barrier for nearly half an hour).

A self-proclaimed non-voter spoke next: "I've made my choice, I'm voting for Zemmour."

Many of those who spoke were former supporters of Marine Le Pen's National Rally. Maxette Pirbakas, a Guadeloupean deputy in the European parliament for France's overseas territories, was one.

"We want our territory to be treated with equity and respect," she said, drawing a few halfhearted cheers.

She was followed by Stéphane Ravier, another National Rally Senator who switched sides to Zemmour. He represents Bouches-du-Rhône, the territory surrounding Marseille. His voice broke hoarsely as he belted out the opening strains of La Marseillaise.

"France will have the last word against all those who want to destroy it! [We have] the right to be proud to be French," he thundered, against those who would "prefer to see France Islamicized."

The crowd roared back, tricolor flags whipping around in the air. "This is our home, this is our home, this is our home!"

"This country that we love," Rivier challenged the crowd, "are we going to let it disappear?"

"NO!!!" they shouted back.

Laurence Trochu came next. She is the president of the *Movement Conservateur*, the right flank of LR which endorsed Zemmour. She was François Fillon's spokesperson during the 2017 primary campaign, and later a member of the political bureau of Les Républicains before joining Zemmour's campaign.

"The family is the beating heart of France," she said. She warned gravely against those who "in the name of progressivism try to deconstruct the French family."

"Taking care of the family," Trouchu said, "is taking care of the entire society." 40 years of immigration and the rise in insecurity had, she went on, threatened daily life. "The war between classes," she said, "has [been] transformed into the war between the sexes. It's time to get rid of this feminism which has reduced feminimity and masculinity to social constructs, this feminism which emasculates men."

At this, chants of "Vive les femmes!" broke out.

"We're the inheritors of a civilization which we love," Trochu finished. "Which we want to protect, and which it's up to us to transmit."

Between some of the speeches, large screens at each side of the stage showed videos of parents whose children had been killed in terrorists attacks or by immigrants. One mother talked about her son, who was killed by an Algerian. He was stabbed 11 times by the man who was in the country illegally.

The crowd angrily talked amongst themselves watching the video.

"Get out!" somebody shouted.

"I put all my hopes in him," the mother said on the screen.

A loud chant broke out: "End migration! End migration! End migration!"

Antoine then leaned over to talk to me. He said he worked with a charity that helps migrants. Still, he said, he didn't see any contradiction between this and supporting Zemmour. "If they don't have a job they have no business being in France."

Jacline Mourad came to prominence through a viral Facebook video in October 2018, where she talked about her opposition to the fuel tax the Macron government was introducing. The video had over 6 million views, and fueled the *Gilets Jaunes* movement. The prime minister at the time, Édouard Philippe, met with her and other members of the movement a month after the video appeared. Today, she's an advisor to Éric Zemmour's campaign.

"How beautiful France is!" she declared, before warning that the French people are treated like "sub-citizens" in their own country.

Zemmour, she said, "is the only candidate." "My support for Éric Zemmour is total," she proclaimed.

"Me too!" somebody shouted out in the crowd.

"Me too!" said another.

Mourad stopped speaking and smiled at the crowd as a brief chant of "us too" broke out.

After she finished her speech, the screen showed another video. A mother told the crowd that "a Sudanese migrant" (here there was a long and steady boo) had murdered her son (the crowd murmured here).

Antoine took this time to tell me a story about how his wife had been a wedding photographer at a Muslim wedding. After she'd shot the wedding, eight months passed before she heard from the bride to pick the photos up. When the bride finally came for them, she only wanted the ones she was in. Her husband had stabbed her in the stomach with a knife, Antoine said.

Here, he explained, meaning France, "there aren't the same rules as in the Maghreb... It's not the same mentality," and "they don't respect it... Not all of course, but certain [ones]." "Faced with people from a different culture," he told me earnestly, "you need penalties... In New York you have zero tolerance." He went on: "There are lots of Moroccans and Maghrebis who are well integrated, and they don't want more immigration."

The next speaker, Jean Messiha, is a perfect example of this sort of assimilation. Messiha was born in Egypt and came to France when he was eight. He didn't speak a word of French, he said. Until the age of 20, when he became a naturalized citizen of France and legally changed his name, he was called

Hossam Boutros Messiha. Messiha is another ex-RN figure
– he left the party in 2020. He was recruited into the party
after meeting with Marine Le Pen because of his background
as a high-ranking civil servant – Deputy Undersecretary of
Management at the Ministry of Defence – and a graduate of
the prestigious École nationale d'administration.

"Like Zemmour," Messiha told the crowd, "I come from
somewhere else." But, he continued, through assimilation he
became French.

Messiha looked at the burning sun in the sky and assured
the crowd that it was "the sunlight of our victory in a few
weeks… I'm fighting so here never becomes somewhere else,
and somewhere else never comes here," he said. "I'm fighting
so France stays what it is: French."

The crowd goes wild, raising what seems like hundreds
of French flags around me. There are no doubt thousands
of flags in the square that day. As they wave around me,
blocking out the sky, it's like being in an enormous tricolor
tent, buffeted by the wind from outside, the roar of the crowd
like jubilant gusts from a mounting storm.

"I'm assimilated," Messiha told the newspaper *Libération*
in 2017. "Arab on the outside, French on the inside."[1]

Then, Vijay Monany spoke. A departmental councilor in
Seine-Saint-Denis, Monay said that "he'd seen the French
people become minorities in their own country, I've seen
the French people be replaced everywhere." The "loss" of
Seine-Saint-Denis, the department with the highest rate of
immigration in France, was a theme which Zemmour returned

to constantly.[2]

Monany denounced the vogue for giving more funds to the suburbs to help them, "as if the *banlieu* needs more subsidies, when it really needs less immigration."

He rejected the idea that the inhabitants of the suburbs were left behind. Instead, he said the suburbs were the "spoiled children of the Republic."

At this point in the day there were burned faces everywhere. Eloe, Witolel's son, had covered his head with a shirt to keep the ultraviolet rays off his face. The euro-deputy Jérôme Rivière called for "dissidence against the globalist movement to abolish borders." A water bottle was being passed around. The section we were in was close to the stage, and it was reserved for those who had been bussed in from other parts of the country. To get into the section we had to give up our water bottles. Eloe took the bottle and drank from it eagerly.

Jean-Frédéric Poisson railed against "the delirium of the propaganda which has installed itself in our schools."

Nicolas Bay promised that Zemmour "will organize the remigration of everyone who has no business being here." This got a huge cheer from the crowd. Once General Secretary of RN from 2014-2017, Bay was suspended from the party earlier this year because of accusations he'd been passing information to Zemmour. He told the crowd at Trocadéro that Marine Le Pen "speaks like the Left" now.

Guillaume Peltier was one of the last people who spoke before Zemmour. As a young man he'd been a member of the youth wing of the National Front. Afterwards, he became Philippe de Villers' protege (de Villiers spoke after him).[3] Peltier was Nicolas Sarkozy's spokesman during the 2007 presidential election. And not long before he joined Zemmour, he was the Vice President of Les Républicains.

"You are the army of shadows, you are the army of light," he told the crowd. This reference to an army of shadows was a classic example of the recuperation of the revolutionary heritage of France which the French far right expertly practices. In French an "army of shadows" is "L'Armée des ombres," also the title of a classic 1969 film directed by Jean-Pierre Melville. That movie tells the story of a group of resistors during World War II. Peltier, then, was presenting the crowd there for Zemmour as heroic members of the Resistance. *L'Armée des ombres* is not just any Resistance film though – it was also one that glorified the role of de Gaulle. Peltier, then, was drawing a link not just between Zemmour's supporters and the Resistance, but between them and de Gaulle's resistance.

"France is not a mirage, it's a rendezvous with history," Peltier said. "We have a rendezvous with France, we have a rendezvous with history."

Phillipe de Villiers came out to a crowd singing him a happy birthday – he called the crowd his birthday president. Born from aristocratic roots, Villiers is a longtime reactionary polemicist. He was a senior civil servant under Chirac, then a perennial politician, running for president twice under a small grouping he led called the Movement for France. In

2007, he endorsed Nicolas Sarkozy. His brother is the general Pierre de Villiers, who resigned from his position as Chief of the General Staff in 2017 over budget cuts Macron tried to implement.

Zemmour, Phillipe de Villiers said, "is the only one who names the real." He warned of "a society of neighbors [being] replaced by a cold society" if mass immigration continued. And he condemned "the racism of the 'cancel culture' which wants to replace France."

Marion Maréchal spoke next, glowing blonde and pregnant at the podium. "How long before France becomes an African country?" she asked. 2060 maybe, she implied. After she spoke, it was Zemmour.

The anticipation built for over five minutes. The eerie rising, triumphant music started up again. Then it switched to something more aggressive and jubilant. Still martial, trumpet stabs swelled and drums blasted. On the video screens, Zemmour became visible marching up to the stage from behind. He crossed past the left wing of the Palais de Chaillot. The crowd lit up – the sound system ignited loudly, a low frequency rumble shook in my ribcage and I could feel the goosebumps on my skin. When Zemmour got to the stage the crowd exploded, flags whipping passionately, with jubilation on the sunburnt faces as the clear blue sky began to fade behind the stage.

Zemmour had his arms raised triumphantly in the air – he reminded me of a wiry, roguish little Nixon more than anything else. He was thrilled by the reception, and who wouldn't be? His impish little smile attested to that, the last bit of his graying hair on the side of his head ruffled almost with excitement. When he spoke he became deadly serious.

"I chose Trocadéro thinking of General de Gaulle," he said. Zemmour invited the support of everybody he could find. "I need Gaullists... I need sovereigntists... I need all the family of the right." "Yes," Zemmour declared, "I need Éric Ciotti. Applaud him."

Ciotti's name was chanted by the crowd.

"Yes, I need Jordan Bardella," Zemmour said. Bardella is Marine Le Pen's young protege, the president of the National Rally and their frequent representative on television.

A chant of "we are the right" followed this call to rally the right.

Valérie Pécresse, though, was not invited. "[She] is a centrist already ready to vote for Emmanuel Macron," Zemmour said.

"Marine Le Pen," Zemmour declared, "is a socialist on the economy." "Don't be afraid of your civilization," he said. "Our ideas are not divisive, only journalists say that...You are the silent France."

The crowd started chanting again. "We love you!"

"Me too," Zemmour replied. "I hope from the bottom of my heart that my parents are proud of me."

"We are proud," the crowd chanted back.

"I put my destiny in your hands," Zemmour said to the crowd, his arms outstretched towards them.

"Thank you," people in the crowd shouted back.

"No, thank you," said Zemmour.

"The truth hurts," somebody shouted.

"I'm not a professional politician," Zemmour went on. "Journalists think that's my weakness. The people think that's my strength... The fear of the end of France," Zemmour empathized, drawing the crowd in as his confederates, "isn't an abstract fear."

"Here, here is France," the crowd chanted.

"They say that I'm hard," Zemmour said. "[That']s because the suffering of my people has made me hard." He went on to pay tribute to Patrick Jardin, the father of Nathalie, who was killed at the terrorist attack on the Bataclan theater in November 2015. He was somewhere in the audience. The crowd cheered and chanted for him.

"Insults become punches," Zemmour warned. "Punches become mortal." He said listening to the stories of parents like Patrick whose children had been killed by migrants had also made him hard. "That which has repulsed me for a long time is resignation. The state must be ashamed," Zemmour declared.

"Macron, murderer, Macron, murderer," the crowd chanted.

"I'm fighting for the reconquest of our identity... The reconquest of serenity in France," Zemmour said. "Remember the words of General de Gaulle when he arrived in London," Zemmour began. Then, despite trying to continue to talk, he was drowned out by the crowd singing La Marseillaise.

When he was able to continue again, Zemmour went on.

"The words were: 'I don't celebrate you coming. You're doing your duty. When France is in anguish, its children must save it.' Today," Zemmour continued, "at Trocadéro, we're doing nothing but our duty."

"We're not fighting for ourselves, we're fighting for our children, and our grandchildren…You no longer recognize the country which you lived in! … I'm speaking about the decline of our army and our industry… Yes, you have reason to be afraid, I understand your nostalgia, but I don't believe in fatalism… I want France to become France again." He asked the crowd to become like they were when they were young once again, to work towards electing him, to help him.

Then, he turned to address taxation and the economy. "I'll lower taxes in a way no president before me ever has," he promised. "Work will finally pay…. I like the state which protects the French people… I like the state which makes peace reign… one euro wasted [by the government] is one euro stolen!"

I saw behind me Witolel was watching Zemmour intently in silent agreement.

Then, Zemmour turned to address French Muslims.

"I respect all religions and all believers," he said. But, he added, "it's not for France to adapt to your culture," but for you to adapt to ours.

"This is our home!" chanted the crowd.

Zemmour accused the left of having abandoned the suburbs to Islamism.

"Collaborators!" chanted the crowd.

"The French people are generous," Zemmour said firmly. "We demand only respect." He went on: "Don't reproduce here what your parents fled!"

The crowd was running ragged now; burned by the sun, thirsty, tired. But they persevered and sang along with Zemmour as he recited lyrics from a Jacques Brel song.

"Assimilation is crying when you hear [that]," Zemmour said. "Assimilation is the inverse of racism... It's not a rejection of a part of yourself but an enrichment."

"I say 'us,'" Zemmour said, demonstrating his own commitment to assimilation, "when I talk of Napoleon's army."

Antoine left early: "Not a false note," he told me.

Zemmour built up a crescendo before he finished.

"Everybody tried to discourage me... The polls, the media..."

"Our families," shouted a man.

But they were all wrong, Zemmour said, just as he'd begun his speech. They'd said he wouldn't be a candidate, they'd said he wouldn't get past 3% in the polls, that he wouldn't get the sponsorships that he needed to run. "They all said it and they were wrong about everything."

This rally, Zemmour had said earlier, was "an *avant-gout* of the surprise that's coming," no matter what the polls said.

He finished his speech explosively: "Above all, above everything, above all else," he declaimed as the crowd lifted off with him, "Vive la France!"

Cannons went off behind the stage, blasting red confetti

into the air. The flakes floated out over the crowd, shimmering. One landed right below my breast pocket. They were followed by a blast of blue, then one of shimmering silver.

Zemmour went down through the front of the crowd, beaming and shaking hands – people rushing forward to shake his hand, to touch him, to be near to him.

I thought of Christian, a craggy old Frenchman I'd talked with earlier who remembered when de Gaulle was president. "It's not radicals who come here, it's people who love France," he'd said. He was from Pontoise, to the North of Paris. He said he'd been at Trocadéro in 2007 for Sarkozy, and it had been just as full. Zemmour, said Christian from Pontoise, "is a man of the right, not the extreme right." Like many attendees, he rejected the idea that Zemmour or his supporters were extremists. He blamed 40 years of indoctrination by the socialists for those who thought otherwise. I asked him if he had any memories of when de Gaulle was president.

"Under de Gaulle, we were more free," Christian said. "Work was everywhere." A chant broke out as we talked. "This is our home," belted out a few people.

"It was less political when I was young."

"An Algerian Berber Jew"

Zemmour was a longtime political journalist for *Le Figaro*, the mainstream conservative newspaper in France. He used this position to build a thriving career as a reactionary television pundit and polemicist, writing bestselling books and appearing regularly on programs. Willing to debate anybody, and talk to anybody, he is absolutely convinced of his own analysis, which represents a coherent and fully-fledged ideological universe. He expounds this worldview regularly on the airwaves, which have long rolled out the red carpet to host him. And that worldview goes out to millions of viewers.

"From the moment when we have two civilizations which are on the same territory, we can't make a culture," Zemmour said during one such television appearance in January 2022.[4]

During another appearance on France 5 he made his nationalist priorities clear.

"First of all, I like the French," he declared. "I will protect the French. If we don't have hierarchy, there isn't a nation. If foreigners have the same rights as the French, there isn't a nation anymore."[5]

To Zemmour, this state of affairs already exists. France is "gangrened" by this "colonization," and "all across France, there are innumerable foreign enclaves which are Islamicized and where people no longer live according to French customs." Those who deny this "deny reality."

For Zemmour, politics is civilizational and martial. Those who accuse him of fomenting civil war or pushing a politics that will "shatter" the country are seen as naive, because the country is already under attack. Marine Le Pen's National Front talks about being submerged by immigration; Zemmour innovates by going a step further – France is not only threatened by this submersion, it is already drowning.

Only by electing Zemmour can the country find salvation, through returning to its roots, to its Catholic identity, to its white, French identity. Zemmour says it often: there is nothing more revolutionary than being reactionary.

Zemmour is also, as he deploys with glee against any accusations of racism, a Jewish man from an Algerian family whose grandfather was a Berber shepherd.

For Zemmour, being French is an honor – for him, colonization was a happy accident that made his ancestors French. Because his ancestors, those "Algerian Berber Jews", were born on French soil, he was French too. And so, for Zemmour, the Empire played nothing but a positive role. He wouldn't defend any of the colonial massacres, he assures his readers, what type of shame would he be heaping on his roots if he did that? But neither would he waste too much time condemning them; history is full of massacres, and in the final analysis, the French Empire gave him a chance he never would have had if he'd stayed in dusty North Africa along the coast of the Mediterranean.

"I benefited from French colonization," he said during a television appearance in March 2022, three weeks before the first round of the presidential election.[6]

"I don't consider colonization to be a crime against humanity. I am not Emmanuel Macron. All people were colonizers and were colonized. The Algerians themselves were colonizers. I'm of Berber origin, I was colonized by the Algerian Arabs who govern the country today. I was then colonized by France. I'll repeat it: I benefited from French colonization. It allowed me to come to Paris, to have access to great French literature, to discover Chateaubriand, Pascal, Victor Hugo... I benefited from French colonization."

Zemmour Today

The most exciting thing in international reaction, Zemmour's rhetoric, success, and oratory provokes rapturous acclaim from the reactionary international which has been ascendant in the West since the fall of the Soviet Union. When the Soviet Union was dissolved on Christmas Day 1991, it unleashed a swarm of fascist and reactionary forces across the West. No longer did the counterweight of Communism exist in Europe. Everything could be permitted as the European social democracies began a headlong rush to the right, their *raison d'etre* gone (to bribe European workers away from Communism with profits looted from their imperial possessions).

Zemmour exists in a world where Fascism is mainstream in Europe, where in Austria a party founded by an SS officer won 26% of the vote in 2017 running on an anti-immigration platform, and entered into a coalition government helmed by mainstream conservatives. And even still, every week, every day even, sees another ostensibly inviolate taboo smashed by Zemmour, to the delight of his followers in France and abroad. In him they have a man who can say it plainly. The problem is not just illegal immigration, for Zemmour, but any immigration. He sees a France with net zero immigration, with a revitalized countryside and a petty urban renaissance of the authentic, original, indigenous French – a civilization that has lasted a millennium, which is supposedly in danger of disappearing.

For this reason, he calls his political movement Reconquête – his goal is not just to conquer the Élysée but the reconquest of those lost parts of France which have been "colonized" by Arabs and Africans. It is the revitalization of those territories of the nation where he says white, Christian France has been chased away and menaced, beaten, robbed, murdered, and slaughtered. This process of destruction and displacement, he says, is constant – one of Zemmour's favorite examples is to point out that the vast majority of phones are robbed by Arabs and Africans, and claim that these robberies exist on the same continuum as the Bataclan terrorist attacks, which he reminds his audience were also committed by Africans and Arabs. "That which we euphemistically call 'delinquency,'" Zemmour wrote in his latest book *La France n'a Pas Dit Son Dernier Mot* (France Hasn't Said its Last Word), is more and more the profound print of a war of civilizations being led on our soil."

Zemmour has two themes which he returns to constantly in his rhetoric, which has expanded in its ambition as he speaks before increasingly crowded meeting rooms across the country. His fight is against *Le Grande Declassment*, an economic phenomenon, and *Le Grand Remplacement*, a demographic one. One necessarily follows from the other. They are intimately linked. There are certain people in control of the state who, Zemmour says, over the past four decades have made a series of decisions which the French people were never consulted on in order to change what France looks like. The question of what France looks like ultimately becomes a question of who rules France, and the inevitable outcome from any demographic change has been what Zemmour describes as the immiseration of the so-called native French – confined to rural quarters or urban neighborhoods, threatened and "gangrened" by the steady demographic advance of the new population. Confronting this is the supreme challenge that faces France – there exist no others of equal importance. It is the task, Zemmour says, of a president, of the leader of the nation. Other concerns, like the economy, or ecology, or health, or education, can be handled by ministers. The president's role, his role, is civilizational.

Zemmour distinguishes himself with precision when he explains what this cultural and demographic question is. This precision earned him the endorsement of Marion Maréchal: "I am here," said Marion, Marine Le Pen's niece, speaking at a rally announcing her support for Zemmour in Toulon in March 2022, "because … I am convinced that the cultural and demographic question is the priority." Maréchal's aunt was long the sole standard-bearer of the reactionary formation in French national politics which calls itself the "patriotic camp," garnering wide support in the polls from these same nationalists. The difference, many of them believe, is that Zemmour says what he believes. Marine Le Pen, they say, no longer does. He says plainly what he means when he says that the "face of France" is changing. The physical face, the skin, the color, the bone underneath the skin, in short, the race of France; Christian, white, Western France, which Zemmour claims is being submerged under a wave of mass immigration. Zemmour views this demographic disequilibrium as a war. It is the ultimate war, the most important military priority for him, because it is no less real than the ones that the French military wages today in the Sahel, West Africa, and the Middle East.

In *France Hasn't Said Its Last Word*, Zemmour writes about a phone call he had with the President of France, Emmanuel Macron, on May 1st, 2020. After sparring back and forth about the extent of the problem Islam poses to France (Macron calls "the problem" in Islam the result of "a small minority of thugs"; Zemmour says that jihadists are "supported by the majority" of French Muslims), Zemmour tells Macron that "the collective unconscious of these Muslim populations is to colonize the old colonizer, and to dominate the infidel in the name of Allah."

When Zemmour says this, Macron pauses for a few seconds. Then Macron agrees with him, but says that if he took this line publicly it would lead to a civil war. Zemmour responds that a civil war is coming either way if the country continues following Macron's politics.

Zemmour warns Macron that "the old colonizer is now

the colonized," and that even Francois Hollande questioned, in a book of interviews published at the end of his political career, "how will we be able to avoid a partition? Because really that's what's happening: partition."[7]

Highlighting the rank hypocrisy of the rotten French political class is one of Zemmour's favorite moves, and he's aided immeasurably by the fact that the French political class truly is a collection of dissembling deadbeats. They say one thing in public, preaching a liberal gospel of *"vivre ensemble"* and singing hosannas to a hollow, tokenized concept of diversity in public life, while in private they share the exact same analyses as he does about race, immigration, and Islam.

According to the French investigative journalist Marc Endeweld, Macron is a prime example of this. Macron is "obsessed with what he himself calls the Great Replacement."[8] This is an obsession for Macron because, he believes, France must remain a majority Christian nation. Endeweld says that Macron has the same analysis as Éric Zemmour, or the reactionary weekly magazine *Valeurs actuelles*, who Macron gave a long interview to in 2019.

Zemmour's message is clear: my analysis is what the great and powerful believe behind closed doors, so it must be true; this truth is so taboo that they will not admit it in public, because they are trying to appeal to the new "replacement" population that has installed itself on French soil today, or because they are held in thrall by an effete liberal electorate that buries their heads in the sand.

Zemmour and the partisans of his party, Reconquête

(named as a transparent reference to the Spanish *Reconquista*, which drove Muslims out of the Iberian Peninsula starting in the 8th Century AD) see the vindication of this idea in the letter Macron wrote to the French people announcing his candidacy. In the letter, Macron lists a set of challenges that the country has faced under his first term as president. They include "threats against our democracies, the rise in inequalities, climate change, demographic transition, and technological transformations." This acknowledgement of a "demographic transition" is proof to Zemmour's supporters that the Great Replacement is happening, though Macron's letter frames this challenge in different terms.

"We won't respond to these challenges by choosing to withdraw or by cultivating nostalgia," Macron writes. And in an implicit, though unnamed challenge to Zemmour, he goes on to say that "the challenge is to construct the France of our children, not to rehash the France of our childhood."[9]

For Zemmour, the Great Replacement is the clear and premeditated consequence of decades of policy by the state, captured by a perverse form of the left with more loyalty to Brussels than France, who have realized that their program has no appeal to the true working class. Faced with this failure, they replaced the proletariat as the heroic figure in their historical cosmogony, exchanging him for the figure of the immigrant. These immigrants – Zemmour focuses his broadsides against Arabs and Africans from the Maghreb and North Africa – logically want to come to France to improve their lives because of the degraded states of their homelands, the reactionary narrative goes. Then, because the French worker has failed the Left as a revolutionary subject, and because the sell-out Right believes they have a pliable subject in immigration, all sides of the political spectrum can use these immigrants towards their own ends; inimical of course, Zemmour, to the interests of the Frenchmen who were there first. So over the past 40 years the political establishment facilitated a massive, overwhelming wave to change the face of France.

Christophe Lefèvre, a regional councilor who shifted his support from Marine Le Pen to Zemmour, says he "can understand those who come to find a better life, we can all understand that. But in fact, no, they come here to impose the way of life which they left." We used to not have this problem, Lefèvre says. France, he explains, has long been a country which takes people in; in turn, they must assimilate. But this no longer happens. Now, Lefèvre says, these populations come to try to impose the way of life of the societies that they fled from onto their new host!

This is especially a problem for France because it is supposedly a country which respects human rights. And because France respects human rights, it can't exist when it becomes overrun by a culture that doesn't, Lefèvre continued. Worse, there are politicians who are encouraging this process against the will of the French people. They do this by installing "Islamists" in key posts to further the spread of this ideology.

"The Great Replacement, we can call it what we want, it's a reality today," says Lefèvre.[10]

You look at demography, he finishes, and in one or two generations, yes, you have a replacement.

So why does Lefèvre support Zemmour over Marine Le Pen? Because, he says, Zemmour more exactly articulates what is in his head. Like many who left Le Pen for Zemmour, he says she changed.

To address all this, Zemmour makes clear that his own policy is to change the face of France. "We must, effectively, re-Frenchify," Zemmour explained in a television interview on C News,[11] the network which made him a star as a TV pundit.

"If we are universalist in France, that's because we were Catholic and Christian," Zemmour continued.[12] Universalism and Catholicism are "the same thing," Zemmour says… "But universalism doesn't mean multiculturalism."

In this same appearance, Zemmour claims that "we can come from wherever in the world and become French," but counterposes being Muslim with being French. The way to accomplish this "becoming French" is not simply through integration, which Zemmour is implacably opposed to as a sop and a lie, but through assimilation. What is assimilation?

"It means to become the same, that means you appropriate the history, that means you appropriate the customs, that means you appropriate the way of living, the taste, the literature, learn the words, the language, the countrysides," Zemmour insists.

But, he says, "there are two major obstacles to assimilation. The first is that the French elites, under American influence, have renounced it for the past 40 years." European influence is also culpable. "You know, of course, that European directive that says that integration is a reciprocal phenomenon, first from the host country? And – me, no, me, I remain…" Zemmour sputters out indignantly at the idea.

"Secondly," he continues, regaining his composure, "effectively we have another problem… We have a population that has come from Arabo-Muslim and African countries. Very numerous, and more so, with a culture very far from the traditional French framework, which is Christian and Greco-Roman. That is an enormous problem."

This is compounded, as Zemmour mentioned before, by the lawless power that has installed itself over France.

"You know, it's in the law – for naturalization, we say that you must be assimilated, that people must be assimilated, so, see, we've always differentiated [between populations]… We've renounced it, that's all."

Zemmour has a solution to this: an implacable struggle by the state against Islam. "We can fight Islam and Islamism and at the same time protect Muslims. Remember, in the 60s, the 70s … there was a totalitarian ideology called Communism. We fought Communism and at the same time Communists weren't persecuted. They had the right to work, they had the right to live normally, they could even work in the civil service, contrary to [as] in Germany. You can see clearly, we can very easily distinguish between the two. So I think that it's this which we must do. But we have to simply hold Muslims accountable, and I think that there are many, I'll repeat, me,

I really offer my hand to Muslims, because they ... have zero interest in Islamicizing the country, because they fled Muslim countries."

Hardly anyone in French political life rejects this framing. Only Jean-Luc Mélenchon, a social democratic politician running for president for a third time, with his own ugly history of chauvinism[13] rejects Zemmour. He doesn't deny a demographic transition is taking place, but celebrates it as part of what he calls a "créolisation" of the country. This "créolisation" "is an alternative to the segmented American-style model of society, and to that of the dominant culture which demands the submission of all others."[14]

Challenging Mélenchon on the popular TV show *Face à Baba*, Zemmour rejected this idea full-throatedly: "me, I say, to be my brother, you have to accept France how it is... I don't reject anybody, I simply say, contrary to you, that I want to preserve the French civilization."

Mélenchon was roundly condemned when he didn't join in a march in support of law enforcement organized by a police union in May of 2021. One politician who did appear in support of the police was Fabien Roussel, the first Communist Party candidate in fifteen years. In the last two elections, they supported Mélenchon. Their last candidate, Marie-George Buffet got just 1.93% of the vote in 2007. It coincided with the rise of the National Front (which after the 2017 election became known as the National Rally. Jean-Marie Le Pen got 10.44 % of the vote, a sharp decline from 2002, but enough to establish the party as a permanent political force in the country. Meanwhile, the Communist Party was fading. It was their worst score in the history of the party, and it was a long time coming. To understand how Zemmour rose, we can look at how the left collapsed in France. Part of that is a short history of the French Communist Party.

From Resistance to Government: Charles de Gaulle and the Failures of the French Communist Party

After the end of the Second World War, the French Communist Party (PCF) ascended to the peak of its influence and power. Their violent and successful resistance to Nazi occupation won them credibility from the French working class as a liberatory force in the country. It also earned them a level of respect from the ruling class. This respect was tempered with fear. The more sophisticated elements of the French ruling class knew that the party had earned itself a legitimacy in France which was impossible to be ignored.

One of the Free French leader Charles de Gaulle's advisers, Jean Moulin, wrote a report on the state of the Resistance early in the war and warned that, "left to its own devices, the Resistance would either fragment into anarchy or end up falling under Communist influence."[15]

The task of the French ruling class was to grapple with the problem of integrating the party into the post-war French state without being controlled by it. The task of the Communists was to figure out how to translate the unprecedented level of confidence into state power. The Party failed at this task, though they did earn significant concessions from the state. Ultimately, despite worries early on, it was the ruling class that succeeded in their task.

They succeeded through a break from their earlier methods of controlling the worker's movement. Rather than just controlling the movement, they captured it. This wasn't exactly a unique innovation. The German Social Democrats in the face of the First World War are the archetypal example of the impotency of a worker's party in power faced with the demands of the nationalistic state. Where France has differed from other nations is in the extraordinarily successful deployment of the country's revolutionary legacy to buttress its governing system and mystify its true nature.

France's much derided military failure in the Second World War was the capitulation of the country's ruling elite before the first bullet was fired. Before war broke out the slogan of the reactionary industrialists and cartels in France was that it was better to have Hitler than the Popular Front Prime Minister Léon Blum. After the war was over the balance of power shifted. Blum remained a staunch anticommunist, but even those who had preferred Hitler to him could no longer avoid reckoning with the PCF. France could no longer immediately destroy its communist party – only the crudest reactionaries advocated that position directly anymore. Charles de Gaulle was a sophisticated reactionary, and chose a more subtle strategy: he integrated them directly into his government.

In certain quarters, Charles de Gaulle has an undeserved reputation as a left-winger – even an anti-imperialist. He certainly launched a few harangues against the American empire, and he is often invoked in political debates today for having taken the country out of NATO's integrated military command. But de Gaulle was a committed partisan of empire: the French empire. He was willing to criticize the American empire if it was profiting at the expense of France. But the French Empire didn't profit at the expense of itself. The success of the French Empire was foundational for de Gaulle. Any criticism of capitalism which he voiced was only ever in service to facilitating the greatness and grandeur of France's Empire. This was all part of de Gaulle's political maneuvering.

These maneuvers were particularly successful because of de Gaulle's penchant for maintaining a firm personal hold on power. He accomplished this through some tricky personal positioning.

Once Paris was liberated he had to name a government, and "Just two political forces were able to oppose the sway of the Communists," wrote Jacques Fauvet in his 1959 history of the IVth Republic. "The socialist party, and General de Gaulle."[16] De Gaulle took these two forces and yoked them to his government. Typical of de Gaulle's maneuvers was his appointment of Adrien Tixier and Georges Bidault to his first cabinet. Bidault, a member of the Resistance who hadn't left the country since 1940, became his minister of Foreign Affairs. Bidault was a Christian Democrat who later would participate in the creation of the National Front.[17] For de Gaulle's minister of the Interior, he chose Adrien Tixier – a socialist who'd spent the entirety of the war in the United States. De Gaulle also chose to take a firm hold of the one force not entirely within his control. The Communist Charles Tillon became Minister of Air. Tillon had a rosy career in the Resistance, from which the French Communist Party derived the basis of its post-war legitimacy. That legitimacy, explained Marie-Claire Lavabre and François Platone, was one in the eyes of both the French working class and of the French ruling class.[18]

Fauvet gives an overview of the condition the state was in at the end of the war in *La IVe Republique*: "Anarchy reigned. The *Comites de la Liberation* were trying to supplant the municipalities and the prefects; they created popular tribunals while the FFI [Forces françaises de l'intérieur] instituted military courts."[19]

De Gaulle had sent commissioners out to each region to serve as the representatives of his government. They were invested with expansive powers including the right to pardon, typically reserved solely for the head of state. Most of these commissioners came from the so-called Free French forces, loyal to de Gaulle during the Resistance and loyal to de Gaulle after the war. Fewer came from the Resistance, where Communist forces were stronger.

The Free French were a force organized by de Gaulle from England. De Gaulle never accepted the armistice, signed on the 22nd of June 1940, when the last government of the Third Republic surrendered to Nazi German forces. The armistice surrendered the Northern half of the country to the Nazis. In the South, a government was established in the city of Vichy. Its leader was Marshal Philippe Pétain – a national hero from the First World War when he led French forces at the battle of Verdun. After the war, he became an influential figure in the French military. De Gaulle himself served as a member of Pétain's staff, though they never liked each other, clashing over questions of military doctrine and personal animosity.

De Gaulle began waging his campaign for the French Empire from the great cities of the colonial possessions. One of his first trips after setting up the Free French offices in London was through the North African possessions whose governors had entered into the adventure of resistance with him. De Gaulle knew the importance of these possessions to French greatness. It was never just enough to liberate metropolitan France, a struggle that was led largely by the Resistance under heavy Communist sway.

"If she doesn't hold Bizerte [a city by the Mediterranean in Tunisia], Mers El Kébir [a Mediterranean port city in Algeria] and Dakar [the capital of Senegal, another port city which juts out into the Atlantic], France won't be a great power anymore," de Gaulle once told an adviser.[20]

For de Gaulle, it was never so much the Nazi part of the occupation that bothered him. It was that France had fallen under German occupation and influence.[21] He was also preoccupied with the idea that the British would use their patronage of him and his forces as a pretext for taking France's colonial possessions. This provoked endless animosity between him and the British. De Gaulle was also never particularly concerned with the domestic policies of Vichy France. Though he was never a vituperative anti-Semite like many of the Catholic conservatives in the milieu he came from, he still recognized and identified with it. After the war, Pétain was sentenced to death and it was only de Gaulle's intervention that commuted the old Marshal's sentence.

Soviet diplomats had a lucid perspective of de Gaulle. In August of 1941, the Vichy government broke relations with the Soviet Union[22] and on September 26th, Ivan Maïski – the Soviet representative, searching for allies – met with de Gaulle in London to exchange letters between the USSR and de Gaulle's nascent provisional government. The Soviet letter underlined "the firm resolution of the Soviet government to assure the full and entire restoration of the independence and the grandeur of France when we are victorious together." But Maïski gave an unflattering description of de Gaulle in his journal. Some of Maïski's insights were proven definitively wrong by what was to come, but Maïski's appraisal of de Gaulle's politics and the circle around him is illuminating:

"De Gaulle's milieu is full of *Cagoulards*.[23] There are surely German agents among them. De Gaulle himself understands nothing about politics, he has sympathy for Fascism of the Italian type and doesn't know how to lead (he argues with everybody). He doesn't have the makings of a leader. That especially makes his entourage more important. There's work to do."

But de Gaulle, despite his acidic personality, did know how to lead. And as in the case of Pétain's post-war pardon, he had a flair for intervention; it was a long-running theme in his history and in the mythology which surrounds him. A situation would exist where the French Empire was confronted with threats to its greatness or integrity, and de Gaulle would arrive as a providential figure to move the stream of history along a different path. For Michel Debré, de Gaulle's first Prime Minister during the Vth Republic, "Gaullism was a 'will to dominate events with the objective of maintaining the influence and authority of France' and a rejection of the idea of a 'movement of history against which we can do nothing.'"[24]

De Gaulle faced just such a moment at the end of the war. The commissioners he'd sent out to represent his nascent government were slipping out of his control. "The commissioners of the Republic themselves," writes Fauvet,

"took initiative without referring to Paris. The Marseille commissioner, [Raymond] Aubrac, froze bank accounts and undertook regional nationalizations! The *gardes patriotique* took the place of the police. Summary executions multiplied. Neither the law nor justice were respected everywhere. Finally, poverty threatened the ruined cities where chaotic communication was an obstacle to providing enough supplies at the threshold of a hard winter."[25]

But de Gaulle was fortunate. He had an "unexpected ally" in the challenge he was faced with to reestablish Republican, Gaullist order: the French Communist Party.

How could this have happened? On the 3rd of November 1944, a Political Bureau of the PCF published a resolution warning that "The Communist Party cannot in any manner be associated with decisions ... to disarm the people in the face of a Hitlerian fifth column which the softness of repression [against] has left intact and powerfully armed."

They were referring to the popular militias known as the Patriotic Militia, or the Patriotic Guard. These militias were an alternative to the police force, and rapidly accrued power to themselves. They had strong internal Communist representation, and represented a nascent and growing alternative to the continuity that de Gaulle represented. As the PCF grew in power and popularity, even the establishment of a popular republic under the leadership of the party became possible.

Jacques Duclos also weighed in on the debate on the role of the *Garde Patriotique* in the new order. Duclos was the highest-ranking PCF official in France after the armistice with the Nazis. He was also the leader of the National Front, a Communist founded organization which sought to assemble all the forces resisting Nazi collaboration together. The National Front was the political arm of the *Francs-tireurs et partisans français*, the Communist-dominated guerilla force which fought against the Nazis.[26] In a report presented to the Paris regional section of the PCF at the end of October

1944, Duclos was unequivocal: "The Patriotic Militia, or the Patriotic Guard, as we tend to call it more and more, was birthed in an insurrectionary battle. It has earned its right to citizenship."

The November 3rd statement by the PCF cited above, published in the party's paper *l'Humanité*, went further, adding that the Patriotic Guard "must remain the vigilant guardian of Republican order at the same time as it must actively occupy [itself] with the military education of the popular masses."

That all changed when the Party found itself faced with the opportunity of integration into the state. The Party "approved the dissolution of the Patriotic Guards ... without even consulting the CNR. (Conseil Nationale de la Résistance)."[27] Maurice Thorez, the exiled party leader, was amnestied and returned to France from Moscow. He immediately began leading a policy of collaboration with de Gaulle's government. In de Gaulle's memoirs, he wrote that "the return of Thorez to the head of the Communist Party may have brought more advantages than inconveniences." Thorez, in de Gaulle's estimation, rendered "service to the public interest on several occasions."[28]

When Thorez returned, he delivered a long report at a session of the central committee of the party from the 21st to the 23rd of January 1945. In his report, Thorez argued for the dissolution of the Patriotic Guards.

"The people have the right and the duty to have their voices heard," Thorez wrote, "but it is the legal authority who must carry out searches, arrests, judgements, and the execution of those judgements."

Thorez then delivered his opinion on the Guard, which had become known as the *Gardes Civiques et républicaines*.

"These groups had their *raisin d'etre* before and during the insurrection against the Hitlerian occupier and his Vichyite accomplices. But the situation now is different, public security must be assured by a regular police force constituted for that reason. The *Gardes Civiques*, and generally all irregular armed groups, must not be maintained any longer."

Thorez dissolved the militias on the orders of Josef Stalin in Moscow. It was on this condition only that de Gaulle would allow Thorez back into the country and amnesty him. De Gaulle and Stalin negotiated a secret agreement where Thorez would be allowed back in provided he could prevent the militias from revolting against de Gaulle. Before Thorez left Moscow, Stalin had supposedly told him to hide away arms, to draw the PCF around him, and to remove de Gaulle from power definitively. Instead, Thorez became Vice-President of the Council of Ministers in the new IVth Republic governments.

The capitulation of the party was complete. In that liminal period between the end of the war and the formal establishment of de Gaulle's power as head of state, de Gaulle had worried that the Communists would take power before he could, and institute a new Commune. Now the communists were in his government, he had a banker at the finance ministry, and he was able to call for unity. Unity meant class collaboration. De Gaulle was comfortable enough now to demand no strikes or division under the new Republic. In September 1945 he refused to receive a representative from the CGT, chastising them for viewing a political role for themselves under the new order. There was a limited place for unions in de Gaulle's France, but it was across a negotiating table being offered terms, not as a collaborator in government or power.

The IVth Republic meant the writing of a new constitution. All constitutions are new social contracts which recognize the balance of class powers in their states. This one was full of social reforms de Gaulle would have preferred not to institute. And he lamented the democratic impulses of the parliament.

"Among the meeting of the five great powers," said de Gaulle of the constituent assembly which wrote the constitution of the IVth French republic, "must France again be the sole which finds its representatives at the mercy of a movement of the Assembly?"[29]

All of these obstacles to de Gaulle's vision of France meant he couldn't stay long at the head of a state whose form he detested.

De Gaulle resigned in January 1946. He said he didn't have the power he needed to govern France; democratic forces had constituted the IVth Republic against him, de Gaulle thought. He couldn't govern until they were removed. De Gaulle hadn't won the peace which he wanted. His vision of France was still yet to come. But he had won an immensely important battle in the offensive against Communism, and from then onwards there was no real moment when it seemed possible that the Communists would take power in France again. The uprising in 1968 is sometimes thought of as a possible inflection point in this direction, but once again the Communists delivered de Gaulle from this crisis through their collaboration.

How did the Party fail to exploit such an opportunity? The post-war glow it accrued from this period is legendary, and its influence remains. It forms the basis, alongside the concessions obtained in 1968, for the social system in France which, degraded as it is, is the envy of progressives in the Western World. Every month, it seemed, more Communists acceded to power with de Gaulle. But just as they found greater and greater representation in de Gaulle's government, their power receded.

The Communist Party in France had the power to take down a government, but it never gained enough strength to form their own government. Only de Gaulle would; he *was* France. In *France Hasn't Said Its Last Word*, Éric Zemmour writes that the most revolutionary thing to be is reactionary. It was de Gaulle who showed this to be true, and who really was revolutionary in his reaction.

The PCF Today

Seine-Saint-Denis used to be home to the prize of French heavy industry – it was also the center of the French

Communist Party in the post-war era. And because of the
jobs in this industry, many Algerian immigrants settled in
this region East and North of Paris after the Second World
War. French capital, expanding at a breakneck pace in the
conditions of a welcome peace, needed more labor than the
domestic market could provide. The 93rd, as Saint-Seine-
Denis is informally known (a reference to its postcode – all of
its municipalities have a code within 93000), was a stronghold
of the "red belt," the cluster of Communist and Socialist run
municipalities surrounding the capital city.

The explosion of post-war industry was the source of the
PCF's popular success. The headquarters of the Confédération
Générale du Travail (CGT), France's second-largest union, are
still in Montreuil, right on the edge of the city's border with
Paris. The CGT, still influential in French politics, was at its
high water mark after the war, and nourished deep links with
the PCF. Organized on a "cell" basis in those years, the PCF
implanted itself in every concentrated industrial workplace
that it could find. The party, wrote Lavabre and Platone,
"intended well and good to confirm their organization and
the nature of the party and to favor the recruitment and the
mobilization of militant workers at their workplaces, which
is to say at the place of the conflict of classes, at the places
where the confrontation between workers and the boss took
place."[30]

By the end of 1978, the party had 28,000 cells across the
country; 10,000 of these were organized within businesses.[31]

At the same time, the 1970s saw a so-called economic crisis

which destroyed the industrial base of the country. Seine-Saint-Denis was hit particularly hard. It was an economic offensive waged by the ruling class to move French production out of the country for lower labor costs. When the businesses left, the PCF cells disappeared too. Their strength became their weakness – even though they had conquered political terrain as a result of their deep implantation into these workplaces, and even though in many places that nominal political power still exists, the social base of their party disappeared. The national prospects of the PCF evaporated. Where they had once had Communist ministers in government in the early days of the IVth Republic, and again under François Mitterrand's socialist government under the Vth Republic in the early years of the 1980s, today they have not even run a presidential candidate in the last two elections. They are no longer a force the French ruling class feels is necessary to even contend with.

It was an inevitable development sped along by the flailing of the Party's leadership who reacted to the changing conditions through further capitulation. Its leader Georges Marchais announced the abandonment of the party's commitment to a "dictatorship of the proletariat" on television at the XXIInd Party conference in 1976.[32] Zemmour waxed lyrical about "the very talented George Marchais" in *France Hasn't Said Its Last Word*, relishing Marchais' rhetorical ability on political talks shows. There were other things about Marchais which Zemmour appreciated. In a speech Marchais gave during the 1981 presidential election, he said

that "because of the presence of around four and a half
million immigrant workers and their families in France, the
continuance of immigration poses grave problems today. We
must stop official and illegal immigration."[33] That same year,
a PCF mayor, Paul Mercieca, bulldozed a worker's housing
center for Malian immigrants in the Parisian suburb Vitry-
Sur-Seine. The PCF justified this decision by claiming that
the mayor of the nearby city of Saint-Maur had clandestinely
chased the Malians out of his own town into Vitry. It was
part of a long-term anticommunist strategy, wrote George
Marchais in a long open letter to the Mosque of Paris, who
had criticized Mercieca's decision, to concentrate immigrants
in poorer, Communist governed municipalities:

> "When this concentration becomes very high ... the
> housing crisis worsens; social housing becomes cruelly
> scarce, and many French families can no longer access
> it. The cost of social assistance necessary for immigrant
> families plunged into misery becomes unbearable for
> the budgets of communes populated by workers and
> employees.[34]

Zemmour grasped upon this gleefully. On a television
program in February 2022, he declared provocatively that
"Georges Marchais spoke exactly like me during the [1981]
presidential campaign ... on immigration... He said exactly
what I say about stopping legal and illegal immigration, on
secularism, on assimilation, on the prohibition of the veil."[35]

The decline of the party continued throughout the 80s

and 90s. Despite having disavowed the dictatorship of the proletariat in 1976, the 1979 introduction of the party's statues still underlined that "the October Revolution showed the proletariat of the entire world the way of the revolutionary class." When the statutes were changed again at the 28th party congress in 1994, the new introduction "made no reference to the founding revolution. The 'leading role of the working class' disappeared, as well as the term 'working class' itself. It was a modification, informal as it was, of the identity which the Party wanted to assume."[36]

The same congress transformed the names of the party's institutions; the Central Committee became the National Committee, the Political Bureau became the National Bureau, and the Secretary General became the National Secretary.[37] It was a clear rejection of Bolshevik nomenclature and an assertion of the party's national role. By the 31st Party Congress in October 2001, there were no longer any references to Lenin or the October Revolution. Organization was opened to "total liberty" at the base, a "radical negation of the previous model."[38] From the end of 1996 until 2001, the party lost a full 50% of its members.[39] The reason was twofold. The party was losing members to the attrition of aging and failing to recruit any new young members.

The PCF occupies a place in French society today of patriotic social engagement, but it plays a derisory role in national political life. The municipal governmental power it has left is concentrated particularly around Paris, in those villages and cities once known as the "Red Suburbs." Their primary role is as loyal implementers of municipal social democracy and the source of some red culture. In Montreuil there is a movie theater owned by the city – it has cheap tickets and a good selection of foreign films – and a public swimming pool named after Maurice Thorez. The party pays tribute to the national narrative of France, canonizing Napoleon or Charles de Gaulle, the Revolution and the Resistance (including here, the "good" Charles de Gaulle) against the reactionary trends that claim them. They name streets after Marx and Lenin, they receive tributes from the Communist Party of Vietnam when a leading member of their party dies, but the municipal newspaper they publish twice a month has an advertisement for a powerful regional real estate firm on its back.

When Jacques Chirac died in 2019, the party published a tribute to him on their website,[40] written by Fabien Roussel, then the Party's National Secretary and now the party's candidate in the 2022 presidential election: "Jacques Chirac was popular," Roussel wrote, "even though he put into place many reforms which were much less so."

Knowing how to show the appropriate amount of deference, mixed with the appropriate amount of dissent – Roussel would have been an eager participant in the role the party played after the war.

Gaullism

While de Gaulle's first resignation was seen as a sign of his relative weakness, he was not a weak figure – or a man who existed independent of the class forces which animated him and facilitated his rise to power. One reason why de Gaulle is so difficult to grasp, and represents so many things to so many different trends in modern French politics, is that de Gaulle was essentially a pragmatist. This pragmatism was not a technocratic pragmatism, that is to say the pragmatism of "what is best for everybody," but a pragmatism that served "the practical needs of the French bourgeoisie," as one writer put it.[41]

Gaullism is not so much an ideology as it is a strategy. The personal foibles and eccentricities of de Gaulle, influenced by his unique political history, sometimes led him down corridors which may have seemed favorable to the left in France. The prime example of this was in 1968, when the Communist Party mobilized for the second time in its post-war history to shore up a government led by de Gaulle. The economic gains which the French working class won from that struggle forestalled galloping political developments which may otherwise have run free. Rather than being a refutation of the idea that affluence had made Marxism obsolete, it was an endorsement.

De Gaulle showed a Machiavellian genius in navigating this path, as he did in many crises that the French bourgeoisie faced in the post-war period. He was the decolonizing colonialist, trusted interlocutor for the bourgeoisie with the trade union movement (who in his youth had supported the banning of trade unions), the impetus for the creation of the

IVth Republic and its destroyer.

The most significant and lasting role which de Gaulle played in France was in the destruction of the potential potency of the parliamentary form. This was a legal avenue which the representatives of the workers' parties in Western Europe exploited heavily, profited from, and derived a growing legitimacy. Gaullism meant trading this democratic influence for the influence of a "seat at the table," where representatives from across the broad spectrum of the workers' movement were consulted to sand down the edges of any sharp corners on France's planned capitalist economy.

Essentially a Bonapartist[42] and a conservative, de Gaulle's credibility and popular appeal derived from his military adventures – the Resistance was a powerful imprimatur of credibility which de Gaulle would carry with him throughout his political career. The alliances which the "adventure of Resistance" forged would also mark de Gaulle. By no means were all members of the French business elite onboard with some of de Gaulle's excesses – but what they did know was that at the end of the day he was their man, no matter how mad he could drive them. This was even true when de Gaulle gave his conditional allies within the trade union movement large concessions. He had an instinctual sophistication born from these uncertain years which taught him that bringing the enemies of the bourgeoisie into the bosom of its state's power was the most effective way to neutralize them.

De Gaulle's Bonapartism was essential to understanding his success. He was a secular saint, which put him in a position where his personal legend made him nigh untouchable to conventional political attacks, and much less at the mercy of traditional political lobbies than another sort of leader. De Gaulle saw himself as embodying France, not just one fraction of its ruling class. France, of course, for de Gaulle was aristocratic, monarchic, glorious – a civilization more eternal than the passing present moment. Preserving France was a cultural and demographic task as much as it was an administrative one.

In 1956, de Gaulle observed that France was prosperous, which after the post-war recovery, it was. "It's for this reason that I don't have much of a chance of returning to power," he said. Two years later chaos reigned. De Gaulle took this moment to implement an economic plan that transformed the direction of post-war France. It started with a shock devaluation of the currency. De Gaulle's goal was to balance the books.

He could accomplish this through a classic attack on labor power while appearing at the same time to support raises and participation for workers.

This attack was in response to the "problem" of Algeria, complicated by France's economic situation. It was complicated by France's relationship to the nascent European Union. In November 1957, the Managing Board of the European Payments Union warned France that it would no longer be able to secure credit from them. France was not living up to commitments it made when it secured previous credit to liberalize trade. A succession of young radical governments in a IVth Republic where governments changed at a dizzying pace did nothing to provide reassurance to the nascent European community.

France was faced with a choice between cutting its military budget or its civil budget – it chose a different path with de Gaulle. He could achieve the necessary reforms which the Payments Union demanded of him without cutting a military budget which he was committed to preserving at all costs.

The franc would be devalued by 17.5% as part of a program liberalizing French commerce. It was "modernization," which meant harsh cuts to everything from farm subsidies to military pensions. The initial form of the plan included cuts in the budget everywhere, but de Gaulle wanted to continue financing colonial forces in Algeria. It was, after all, the reason he was in power. So new, steep taxes were introduced on tobacco and alcohol, and prices were increased on postage, energy, and transportation.[43] This reorganization of France's economy inaugurated De Gaulle's role as head of state.

"The French will shout," de Gaulle told his economic adviser Roger Goetze. "So what?"[44]

De Gaulle and Algeria

De Gaulle took these measures to confront the Algerian crisis, which had begun with a revolutionary movement in November 1954.

The so-called crisis was produced by the nationalist,

anti-colonial movement in Algeria coming into contact
with a counter-revolutionary one led by French officers in
the French Algerian military who refused to accept Algerian
secession. While de Gaulle eventually did recognize the need
for Algerian independence, it was not because of any belief
in decolonization. Ultimately, de Gaulle decided that Algeria
was a distraction from the military goal which he thought was
most necessary to preserve France's military independence:
the development of nuclear weapons. France's first nuclear
tests were in the Sahara Desert, part of Algeria's territory. The
local population was given essentially no protection against
these tests.[45]

De Gaulle's fundamental nature was pragmatic and
adaptable. But his eventual recognition of Algerian
independence earned him a hated position as the betrayer of
the French extreme right, many of whom had agitated for his
return to power because of his capacity to keep Algeria.

His return to power had come under the threat of a coup
d'état. There were even some officers in the French military
who discussed landing paratroopers in Paris to take control
of the government. In Zemmour's bestselling book *Le Suicide
français* (The French Suicide), he writes that "the return of
General de Gaulle to power was a legal coup d'état that
succeeded, an 18th *brumaire* which wouldn't need a 19th and
Murat chasing the deputies out of the window."[46]

Zemmour compared de Gaulle's task in Algeria at the end
of the Second World War to Napoleon's role in the shadow
of the Seven Years' War in 1763. "The two men had to restore

the prestige of French power after defeats that were believed [to be] definitive," Zemmour wrote.

De Gaulle organized a referendum for the 8th of January 1961 on self-determination for Algeria. This nearly immediately provoked the formation of the Organisation Armée Secrète (OAS), which began a terrorist campaign to keep Algeria under French colonial rule. The group killed around 2,000 people in their campaign to fulfill their slogan: "Algeria is French and will remain so."

Jean-Marie Le Pen was then a deputy in the French National Assembly. He put forward a motion to recognize the OAS as a legal organization. That failed, but in November 1961 Georges Bidault set up a *Conseil national de la Résistance* for Algeria. The name is provocative – the same as the Resistance organization during the Second World War. Bidault, once de Gaulle's foreign minister, had also been the head of de Gaulle's resistance organization during the war. The Resistance was over now though, and Bidault was required to find new allies among his former opponents.

Raoul Salan was named commander in chief of the new CNR, charged with fighting "against the abandonment of Algeria, Gaullist dictatorship and international Communism." Salan had fought in Indochina, and in 1958 was part of the group of officers in Algeria pressuring the French government to oppose independence. But during the Second World War he had been on the other side of de Gaulle. He had been tasked by the Vichy government with defending Dakar. It wouldn't take him long to find his way back to opposition to de Gaulle.

First though, there was the Algerian crisis to resolve. Salan was made army commander, tasked with fighting the Algerian National Liberation Front (NLF). Then, after de Gaulle's betrayal, and as a leader of the new CNR, Salan led a fight that was half clandestine, half open, violently persecuted by the OAS, and which still has an enduring influence on French political life.

Algeria was different from other French colonies: home to a million French settlers who saw themselves as the true builders of the country, it gained its independence in 1962 in a referendum on July 1st, ratifying an accord made in March in Évian. The referendum had the support of 99.72 percent of the Algerian population. Salan's resistance to independence was futile – he was captured by April 1962 and sentenced to death. That penalty was commuted to life in prison, and he was pardoned by 1968. He died in 1984 as France's most decorated military officer.

In the meantime, the reaction to independence from the pro-French Algerians was violent. In the reactionary narrative, France had built Algeria. If Algeria could not be French, then, these same French saw that it was their task to destroy Algeria, returning it to the state that they claimed it had been found in. Riots broke out with infrastructure destroyed and Algerians summarily executed. Algeria convulsed under the rage of both camps as independence became a fact.

But de Gaulle could breathe a sigh of relief. He'd never wanted an independent Algeria when he came to power

– he was far more interested in the country being a semi-autonomous member of a French confederation, something like the French Union which had been the first French-led attempt at grappling with African demands for independence. Still, one thing he was adamant about avoiding was integration. De Gaulle wanted the territory of Algeria, its resources, and the French empire for which it had become a symbol. What he didn't want was the Algerian and the French communities being on an equal footing. That would mean 80 Muslim deputies in the National Assembly.

It would be wrong to say that the Imperial nostalgics like Zemmour or Jean-Marie Le Pen, who lament the loss of French Algeria, are hypocrites if their authentic concern is the Islamization of the country. Jean-Marie Le Pen never saw a French Algeria where the French and Algerian communities were on an equal national footing. But when a wave of pro-French Algerians (whose militias were known as *harkis*) and settlers (known as *pied-noirs*) fled across the Mediterranean to the South of France, Le Pen could build his political career simultaneously condemning the North African workers who provided cheap labor for French factories and by courting the *pied-noirs*. This former settler population, along with the *harkis*, still leaves an important mark on French political life. Romance for a French Algeria hasn't disappeared – people like Zemmour are only the most vocal representatives of it. France had "lost" Algeria to dark forces that represented the termination of the empire and a fall into Communism and Islamism. For de Gaulle it was particularly painful: "me, who was brought up in the religion of the flag, of French Algeria, of the army as guarantor of the Empire."

Algeria, to the settlers and officers who led the *Algérie Française* movement, *was* France. And indivisibly so. The Mediterranean that separated the Algerian department from the metropole was no different than the river Seine which flowed through Paris. In their minds, it was the French settlers who had built Algeria. After all, they pointed out, Algeria had been French since 1830 – Nice only became French in 1859. For these settlers, they had not just built a colony but an integral part of the nation. When the French mainland fell to the Nazi invaders during the Second World War, there was talk about fleeing to French North Africa to continue the war. This was no different to those who proposed it than previous retreats of the government to Bordeaux, or a planned defense of Brittany.

Thus, Bidault could see the struggle he was waging to keep French Algeria through the same lens of the resistance that he had entered into two decades before. To many, the loss of French Algeria was "even more traumatic than France's defeat by Germany in 1940."[47]

De Gaulle's thinking on Algeria changed over time. But "de Gaulle never believed in 'integration' nor did he welcome it," wrote Justin Jackson. There was the problem of the Muslim deputies, no doubt. More than that though, there were the Muslims themselves. There were 9 million of them, at a time when the French population was just 45 million. The *pied-noirs*, at first hostile to any idea of integration, became more amenable to the idea when they saw it as their only way to remain in power. But de Gaulle never supported integration of the Muslim population because he was a racist. "Have you seen the Muslims with their turbans and their djellabas?"[48] de Gaulle once asked his trusted adviser Alain Peyrefitte.

> "You can see that they are not French. Try and integrate oil and vinegar. Shake the bottle. After a moment they separate again. The Arabs are Arabs, the French are French. Do you think that the French can absorb ten million Muslims who will tomorrow be twenty million and after tomorrow forty? If we carry out integration, if all the Berbers and Arabs of Algeria were regarded as French, how would one stop them coming to settle on the mainland where the standard of living is so much higher? My village would no longer be called Colombey-les-deux-Eglises [Churches], but Colombey-the-two-Mosques."[49]

Zemmour often quotes this passage which appears in one of Alain Peyefritte's memoirs. In *France Hasn't Said Its Last Word*, he explains how his late friend Philippe Séguin (once president of the National Assembly), though a Gaullist, never understood that de Gaulle had given Algeria its independence so he could preserve his village's demographic character. And against Séguin, who Zemmour says believed that Maghrebi immigrants could be integrated, Zemmour quotes de Gaulle on Arabs and Frenchmen, oil and vinegar. De Gaulle could be even more crass and inflammatory.

"Do you want to be n****rified?" he asked the deputy

Raymond Dronne mockingly as he dismissed the idea of integration.[50]

"De Gaulle's opposition to integration [was] 'racist,'" acknowledged Jackson dryly.[51]

When de Gaulle "lost" Algeria, it represented the beginning of the end for the France that was. Éric Zemmour's bestselling 2016 book *The French Suicide* begins on the day of de Gaulle's funeral, November 12th, 1970. "In Zemmour's noxious narrative," writes Jackson in his 2018 biography of de Gaulle, "de Gaulle's death opened the floodgates to all the ills (as he sees them) of contemporary France–national decline, feminism, homosexuality, mass immigration."

In that book, Zemmour praised Richard Nixon for recognizing this greatness in de Gaulle.

"In a plane transporting him to Paris on the 11th of November 1970," wrote Zemmour,

"the American President Richard Nixon confided to several journalists that de Gaulle was one of those rare men of the world where we are able to say that he was greater than the power he represented. Nixon knew Eisenhower, Churchill, Adenauer, and de Gaulle. 'All four of them were equally giants,' he said, 'But it was probably de Gaulle who had the most difficult task: France wasn't dead, but its soul was virtually dead. De Gaulle took in his hands the destiny of a people whose soul was virtually dead... Only his will and his determination was able to keep this soul alive... The only man who was able to save France from a civil war between 1958 and 1962 was Charles de Gaulle. France would not exist anymore as a nation without him.'"

"Nixon, in his overflowing admiration," Zemmour finishes approvingly, "saw fair and long." Again, in Zemmour's discourse, the threat of civil war rears its head. In fact, it is here, but who can deliver France from it? The French Empire that produced de Gaulle, its last defender, no longer exists; Algeria killed it, and de Gaulle is no longer around. The loss of Algeria was also the loss of the French Empire which produced Éric Zemmour, but Zemmour is still here.

De Gaulle was no great decolonizer – he simply presided over the French Empire in the age of decolonization. Decolonization was happening – it was a historical fact, and de Gaulle knew some recognition of national independence couldn't be avoided. What could be determined was the shape decolonization took.

De Gaulle had handled the crisis in a sophisticated way – he took the losses which France couldn't avoid, and held on to as much as he could. De Gaulle realized early on that the French Empire couldn't look the same and still endure. His solution was a reorganization of the French Empire. The roots of this realization and decision were in February of 1944, when the governors of the French colonial territories held a conference and formally abolished the colonies. They were transformed into the "French Union," and became "integrated territories," parts of the French nation themselves. It was this decision that made Algeria not simply just a colony, but France.

The African Union gave way to the French Community. The Community granted its member-nations some limited control of their internal affairs. It was a limited, devolved autonomy. Paris still held their currency reserves in France, which also continued to print the currency, called the CFA Franc, of many of the West African states. This remains the case today, and essentially blocks these countries from developing a sovereign monetary policy of their own.

Under the French Community, member states had internal legislative and executive Branches but the military, foreign, economic, and fiscal policies – as well as their justice systems – remained in the hands of the executive of the community. That executive, of course, was France. De Gaulle's great decolonization meant something very different from true independence in French Africa: in 1979, France still dominated their economies.

A study of France's role in Africa in *Dirty Work 2: The CIA in Africa*, explained what this control looked like:

"Economic dominance in client nations can be typified by considering the percentage of the modern sector of the economy controlled by the dominant nation. For France, in the case of the Ivory Coast, it is 50 percent; in Cameroon, 55 percent; in Senegal, 57 percent; and in Gabon, 65 percent. Moreover, these client nations supply at low prices the raw materials that are absolutely necessary for the survival of the French economy: aluminum from

Cameroon, phosphates from Senegal, oil from Gabon, and uranium from Niger. One of these client nations, Upper Volta,[52] is in fact the poorest of all Africa, with ninety dollars per capita average income in 1975. The loss of this economic dominance would certainly bring about great changes in France itself, and that is why the regimes of those client nations are so firmly supported in spite of their corrupt and often repressive nature."[53]

This explains the modern French preoccupation with nuclear power. Why does France use so much? Is it the fruit of an enlightened, rational civilization utilizing cutting edge energy technology, and unwilling to bend to superstitious anti-nuclear dogmas? Or is it because France gets cheap uranium from Niger? The safety and efficacy of nuclear power is a question for another work, but Nigerian uranium is not. France has cheaper electricity bills than England. This is in no small part because France controls the economies of its former colonies to a much greater degree. And this reason is no small part why Éric Zemmour and the whole reactionary spectrum in France delivers panegyrics to nuclear power. It gives them an easy "win" over ecologists too timid to trust nuclear power, and it also lets them remind the world that France is a great power.

France's success with nuclear power is unique because nuclear power is uniquely affordable to France.

In 2013, the French state-owned mining company Areva, which mines uranium in Niger, had global revenues of

$13 billion. That was twice the size of the entire Nigerien economy. Before a contract renegotiation, Areva paid royalties of 5.5% of its mines. At the same time in Canada, its royalties were 13% – in Kazakhstan they were 18.5%. France uses 8,200 tons of uranium per year to generate electricity. Most of it comes from Canada and Niger. Despite providing the uranium which powers one out of every three lightbulbs in France, just 10% of the population of Niger has reliable access to electricity. In rural areas, the number tumbles to 1%.

Though the French Empire is formally gone, France still enjoys a neocolonial relationship with Africa it has an interest in maintaining. If it doesn't, the quality of life in metropolitan France would undoubtedly be lower. France largely maintains its power in Francafrique through interlocking personal and financial relationships with local elites (Nicolas Sarkozy, for instance, presided over the marriage of the Ivorian IMF economist Alassane Ouattara – who in 2010 he became president of the Ivory Coast). But it also maintains a large and active military contingent on the continent, the true extent of which is outside the scope of this book. Suffice to say that Zemmour is no opponent of it.

Zemmour's Foreign Policy

After Russia invaded Ukraine in February 2022, Éric Zemmour gave a speech on the subject of peace. Zemmour has long been a critic of NATO, following France's long tradition of pseudo-independence from the bloc. Charles de Gaulle took the country out of the alliance's integrated military command structure in 1966 in part to avoid purchasing obligations from American manufacturers so he could build up the French arms industry. Despite this posturing, France never actually left the alliance, and negotiated secret agreements with the alliance to continue cooperation in the event of a war.

In 2009, Nicolas Sarkozy brought France back into NATO. Zemmour thinks this was a terrible mistake, not least because it degrades France's war industry, and limits its independence in geopolitics. In the days before and after the Russian invasion of Ukraine, Zemmour spoke out against NATO pressure on the country, echoing a familiar critique to those in the anti-imperialist camp. Russia had been promised on the dissolution of the Soviet Union that NATO would halt its Eastward expansion. Instead, the Western powers had sought to encircle Russia, particularly after Vladimir Putin came to power and charted an independent, sovereign course. But for the anti-imperialist left, this is where the similarities end.

Zemmour has a criticism of the European Union that blends a standard left-populist laundry list ("austerity, reduced salaries, mass unemployment, poverty and, even better, forced exile in East Germany to work hard ... in vast food farms," he writes in *Un quinquennat pour rien*)[54] with a reactionary right-wing critique of the European Union. In the East of Ukraine there lives, he writes, "an important Russophone minority. These feel closer to their ancient Russian ally and master.

They have no desire to cozy up with a Western Europe they see as a decadent land, undermined by multiculturalism, insolent irreligiosity and militant homosexuality."

This is the standard reactionary strain of support for Putin's Russia from the reactionary right, which bats at anti-imperialism as a style, not a practice. It's a syncretic gesture that obscures their true intentions. Zemmour opposes NATO: this is true in a limited sense, and he does want to remove France from the integrated military command structure. But what does this mean for France? Zemmour gave a speech at Mont Saint-Michel shortly after the release of his defense policy. The rhetoric of the speech and the fine print of the policy show Zemmour heading down a different path. Yes, France will leave NATO, just as de Gaulle did. But was de Gaulle an anti-imperialist figure? Hopefully this book has answered that question by now. The short answer is no. And as usual, Zemmour follows de Gaulle.

Zemmour spoke in Mont Saint-Michel about rebuilding a France of "power" – his speech also introduced the idea of a "Gaullism of Reconquest." This is Zemmour's foreign policy paradigm, a reconquest of French weight on the world stage. NATO's greatest sin is to make France play second fiddle to America. America is to be opposed not for its imperial adventuring, but because it is a rival in that imperial adventure. Hence Zemmour's wish to revitalize French heavy industry by exiting NATO. Disengaging from NATO is an administrative reorganization of the French Empire, for Zemmour, not a proposition to end it.

In fact, Zemmour will extend the reach of the French Empire, and continue its dominance over the African continent. His Defense policy calls for recruiting 50,000 more soldiers. Then, starting in 2023, Zemmour will raise the budget by €3.6 billion a year. The goal will be to have a defense budget of €70 billion by 2030. Zemmour's *Immigration Zero* goal will reduce net immigration in France to zero. Meanwhile, troops in France's African military bases will be doubled, from 7,000 now to 14,000 by 2027.

At Zemmour's so-called peace rally, he used the war in Ukraine to demonstrate his perspective on borders: "with this war, borders will finally henceforth be perceived for what they are: indispensable guarantors of liberty, of security, and of peace between peoples."

In Russia's imperial adventure, he sees a lesson for France. The world is harsh. Europe is a lie, and provides no protection against war. "The next President must reestablish [France's] sovereignty wherever it's necessary. He must protect her borders like a precious treasure. He must reinforce its army but also her police and her courts."

The dream of Empire never really died for Zemmour. But with the exterior the French Empire gone and decolonization advancing again through the academy – a malign import of the American ideology of "*wokisme*" – what remains and what's to come? For Zemmour and his partisans, it is a civil war. A reality and a prophecy.

The Officers' Letter

Zemmour is not alone in prophesying an imminent civil war. There is once again a faction in the French military which believes the country faces this threat. On one side of this war, there are the forces of the Republic, of traditional France, the Church, the traditional institutions of the countryside and this military faction; on the other are, according to nationalists, the creeping forces of Islamism aided by the sellout traitors of the left and actively malevolent foot soldiers of Islamo-leftism in the academy.

Faced with this threat of Islamic separatism, these generals and young officers are once again preparing to join a project of political disobedience. This choice of resistance is perceived by these officers to be similar to the one which the officers who followed de Gaulle made in 1940. The lessons these young officers learned from '40-'45 were then put to use in '58 when the greatest and most enduring scar of "separatism" was opened – the secession, declaration of independence, and decolonization of Algeria.

The choice of resistance for French officers then was bound up in two different conceptions of loyalty – it was necessarily a political choice. Officers who viewed themselves as non-partisan servants of the institution of the military were incapable of exercising any sort of neutrality in such a situation.

French officers "Had for themselves a choice to make, a difficult choice," explained Jacques Fauvet.[55] They could continue swearing obedience to their chain of command and the legitimate government, or they could choose a "national duty" and join the Free French under de Gaulle. Their choice, then, was to "continue the war with de Gaulle, or accept peace with Pétain."

This choice, according to Fauvet, was the germ of disobedience which the infected officers would carry to 1958, when they again chose to defy the traditional chain of command to bring de Gaulle to power during the Algerian crisis.

"It was here that the officers learned to disobey, to consider dissidence a duty. Their engagement was first of all military, national; it quickly became political."

The great adventure of de Gaulle, then, was one that transformed the French military, "that of the numerous young officers who later became the generals of the IVth Republic. It was in 1940-42 that the generals and the colonels of 1958 learned disobedience and politics."

"This reason," continued Fauvet, "can be added to others to explain the coup of May 13th in Alger."

"They learned politics twice [these young parachutist regiment commanding officers who all made war in Africa with de Gaulle, then without him in Indochina]: that which they inculcated the Gaullist movement with from 1940-1945, and the lessons they took from the revolutionary war of the Viet Minh."[56]

"Weak in metropolitan opinion, inexistant in political milieus, Gaullism would have been unable to be reborn in

France without the events in Alger," finished Fauvet.

It's in fertile ground similar to this which Zemmour's neo-Gaullism can take root. There is the perception of a threat to France as a unitary entity which animates every follower of Zemmour and Zemmour himself. The nation and the very idea of France, they say, is under attack:

"Monsieur President,
Mesdames, Messieurs of the government,
Mesdames, Messieurs members of parliament

"The situation is serious, France is in peril, it is threatened by many mortal dangers. Us who, even while retired, remain soldiers of France, cannot, in the current circumstances, remain indifferent to the fate of our beautiful country."

So begins a letter published in April of 2021 on the site Place D'armes, a forum for French military veterans.[57] "Today, there are those who talk about racialism, indigenism and decolonial theories," the letter charges. But these are all euphemisms for a "racial war that these hateful and fanatic partisans want."

"They disrespect our country, its traditions, its culture, and want to see it dissolved by tearing out its past and its history."

The disintegration produced by this, claims the letter, is coming about because of "a certain antiracism," which in reality has one "sole goal: to create on our soil a malaise, even a hatred between communities."

The warning these generals issue isn't simply that the values of the French people have been changed, but that the very territory of the country is being divided in two. A splintering of the unified nation is being produced as France fractures into different communities on French national soil. The letter continues its warning about the disintegration taking place,

"With Islamism and the hordes of the *banlieue*[58] carrying out the detachment of multiple parcels of the nation to transform them into territories subjected to dogmas contrary to our constitution. But every Frenchman, whatever his belief or nonbelief is, should be at home everywhere in the Hexagone;[59] there should not be able, and must not be able to exist any city, any neighborhood where the laws of the Republic don't apply."

What these officers are saying, of course, is that there are already cities and neighborhoods where the laws do not apply. This is a staple of any right-wing media diet nowadays: the British press calls them no-go zones, American talk radio warns of creeping Sharia, and the French media has turned reports on them into a cottage industry. Seine-Saint-Denis is the example par excellence in this drama: Seine-Saint-Denis is a county to the North and East of Paris where many Arab and North African immigrants and those of Arab and North African heritage live.

These cities and villages were once known as the "red belt," because they represented the bulk of French Communist Party local power, with town halls and municipalities governed by the party for decades – in some places over half a century.

Zemmour was born in one of these cities, Montreuil, popularly and not always derisively known these days as "Mali-Sous-Bois," because of its large West African immigrant, and particularly Malian, population. Though Montreuil is its own city with a population of around 110,000 people, it is considered, like many of the towns right outside the Paris borders, as an adjunct of the city, the suburb where the traditional working class, poor, and immigrants live as they strive to make it to Paris.

Zemmour was born in Montreuil then grew up in Drancy, a suburb to the North. As he gained media success, he traded the suburbs for a bourgeois, semi-aristocratic West Parisian life of letters. Just as he abandoned the suburbs, French capital left too, leaving a hollowed out, deindustrialized wasteland. Unemployment in the 93rd reaches staggering levels among the young, particularly in the Northern ring capping Paris. But these suburbs are owed nothing, Zemmour says. The true France lives elsewhere.

The Fight for the Countryside

One of Zemmour's campaign themes has been to revitalize rural France. He stands here most starkly in opposition to the "center-right" Valérie Pécresse. She is the regional president of Île-de-France, home to Paris and its hated suburbs. Pécresse, the candidate for the mainstream, traditional right-wing party "Les Républicains," is the symbol of this metropolis and its blend of a pro-European, traitorous Right which only Zemmour, he himself believes, can save and return honor to.

The cities and suburbs are the home of the Great Replacement, that land which is nearly lost. These suburbs, particularly to the East and the North, aren't the leafy idyllic burgs of the American suburban imagination. Today, they are the vast, impoverished repositories of an immigrant population that once staffed the factories which circled Paris in a ring called the *couronne*, or crown. Now, in a deindustrialized France, it provides the labor power for the Parisian kitchens in the West Parisian restaurants haunted by the old bourgeoisie of the city.

They are also the vanguard of the Islamization of France, warns Zemmour, where local governments submit to the demands of the new populations, approving permits for mosques, allowing religious instruction, and tolerating the wearing of the veil.

But rural towns, Zemmour imagines in a sort of Maoist war of position, can encircle these now lost cities and suburbs. Then, with time bought by a campaign of mass deportations and pro-natalist policies for the indigenous French population, they can win back these towns and restore them to what France once was. These are the Frenchmen Zemmour tries his hardest to talk to, their inhabitants, the new *Maquis* who are waging a mighty and heroic resistance against the forces of globalization who were themselves so certain they had won a final victory.

This brings us to another artful way that Zemmour and his

reactionary cohort talk. The *Maquis* were rural guerillas who
fought the Nazi occupation during the Second World War.
Nobody has ever been better than the French at rehabilitating
the country's revolutionary heritage towards reactionary ends.
For Zemmour and the fascists who tail him, anybody who
denies the threat of Islam or the demographic menace of
Arab and African immigration, is a collaborator. If you march
with Muslims against the rising atmosphere of hate again
Muslim citizens, you are a "collabo."

In *France Hasn't Said Its Last Word*, Zemmour writes
about his meeting in 2011 with Renaud Camus, a polemicist
who has written extensively about the Great Replacement.
Zemmour comes away from this meeting with nothing but
respect and admiration for the erudition of Camus, who he
finds charming and charismatic. Camus "had an exemplary
distinction, an aristocratic humility, and a devastating sense
of humor," Zemmour gushes. He compares this meeting
with one he had the same year with Pierre Bellanger, a rap
producer. For Bellanger, sneers Zemmour, "rap is his thing.
His ray of sunlight." Bellanger explains to Zemmour that the
new population of the suburbs have to be given their "musical
pittance," in Zemmour's words.

After his meeting with Bellanger and Camus, Zemmour
says that "it was as if in 1942, I'd met a collabo followed
by a member of the resistance." For Zemmour, France is
already occupied. Those who provide cultural comfort to the
enemy by diffusing rap music (for Zemmour, an "illiterate
sub-culture") are comparable to Nazi occupiers, and those

who name the "problem" of "demographic subversion" are resistance fighters. Zemmour sees himself as leading that resistance, ready to once again liberate the countryside from an evil occupation.

One policy Zemmour has announced to take back the countryside is a grant of 10,000 euros for every new baby born to a French family. The criteria for eligibility for this grant, says his team, are those that *Insee*, the governmental bureau of statistics, uses for determining "rurality."

Insee has a sophisticated set of criteria for determining whether a place is rural or not. One criterion they included before refining their methodology in 2020 was the raw population of a town. If it was under 2,000, it was rural. Today, they also include things like how much influence a large nearby city has on the town, or how isolated and autonomous it is.

But Zemmour's conception of the countryside is less based in methodological sophistication than it is in a mythology about what the true France is. At the same time, Zemmour and his spokesmen use these statistical definitions to counter charges that there's anything racist about a grant designated solely for French babies born in the countryside. They say that all this does is restore equilibrium to a system of social spending which for far too long has been preoccupied with taking care of the suburbs and the cities. The "*prime de naissance*," then, simply corrects a financial imbalance created by a system which cares far more about the core than the periphery. The policy, says Zemmour, is part of a "true politics of natality and reconquest of the countryside."

Is this lavish social spending and a statist turn by Zemmour? The money can be spent on anything – childcare, transportation, baby formula. Could it be part of an ambitious program of social spending by a candidate of the right who doesn't reject the role of the state in the economy, a true Colbertist, as he calls himself?[60]

It is a promise of social spending. But at the same time, Zemmour promises to cut the amount of social housing in the countryside, by repealing a law which requires 25% of each new housing development to be social housing. Social housing, for Zemmour, means immigrants. "Between 20 to 30 percent of social housing demands are made by foreigners," he sneered. The government "[doesn't] give precise figures, not to shock the French."

Zemmour, then, is open to some social spending. But only for the "true French." He says he will protect France's social welfare system even as he promises to cut it, all the better to root out the foreigners lurking within it. This is a feature of the new Fascism sweeping over Europe. They will not reject the state or embrace the market. For them, the state is a powerful tool they can use to transform their nations into their ideal societies: ethnically and culturally homogenous, low-tax, militarized police states.

The "*prime de naissance*" is an example of this. It doesn't apply to just any baby born in the countryside. Instead, it's reserved for "true" French babies – meaning babies born to two parents of French nationality. Defending the policy in a morning interview with Appoline Malherbe on RMC France, Guillame Peliter, Zemmour's spokesman – the former LR vice-president – said nationality has nothing to do with skin color or country of nationality. But he said that when people come to France they need to make a choice – binationals will no longer be permitted.

And nationality necessarily has *something* to do with skin color when Zemmour also proposes ending birthright citizenship; nationality is no longer something anybody can get when it becomes a question of blood right. Of course, that's Zemmour's aim anyway.

Zemmour's reconquest is necessarily demographic, and he makes no attempt to hide this. This is his appeal, and this is his program. Every social program he proposes is part and parcel of an attempt to demographically transform France.

Spend any amount of time talking with officials in the National Rally and in Reconquête and you will inevitably discuss the Great Replacement. They all say it's not merely a theory, but a fact and a reality. One National Rally youth official defended himself against the charge of conspiracism and tried to differentiate himself from Zemmour. He didn't believe the process was directed by the state. Still, he said, it was a statistical reality, with consequences, that the state must address.

"Every time that someone is intimidated ... in the street, it's always, systematically, the same profile," Enzo Alias, the National Delegate for International Relations in the National

Rally's Youth Wing, said in February 2022.[61] "So, obviously, immigration is linked to insecurity because the state hasn't done its job to assimilate a certain part of the population which has come to install itself in France. So you have an entire part of society, which comes from immigration, which is permitted to not respect the country, to not respect the law, and to not respect the French people in general."

The Great Replacement is a fact for Alias, like most of his fellow members of Rassemblement National. Zemmour's strategy is to address this phantasm by proposing doing something about it.

Part of the reason for Zemmour introducing policies aimed at rural voters is that the countryside is the base of Marine Le Pen's support. One functionary in the National Rally said that people in the countryside think less about the Great Replacement, because they live in areas with much less immigration. In the cities, they say, the Great Replacement is a self-evident fact, and so the discourse of security, ending crime, and reversing this trend is enough to appeal to the right-wing constituency available to Zemmour. To take hegemony over the right, Zemmour needs the countryside. To do that, Zemmour needs to knock out Le Pen.

A Civil War on the Right

Zemmour candidacy is one product of the schism with the "patriotic camp," which until now was represented in France solely by the National Front and the Le Pens. After the Second World War the reactionary right wing's reputation was tarred with Nazi collaboration. The patriotic camp rejected this guilt and asserted its reaction proudly. Their conservatism is deeply grounded in the strains of Royalism which still runs through French politics, in a racist defense of a white, Catholic Europe they see under siege, and in a fanatical anticommunism.

In 2002, Jean-Marie Le Pen reached the second round of the presidential election. It was the first time what the French media calls the "Extreme Right" accomplished this under the Vth Republic. The result was a shock – a duel between the Socialist prime minister, Lionel Jospin, and the president Jacques Chirac had widely been expected. But Jean-Marie Le Pen won a little less than 200,000 more votes than Jospin, enough for him to make it into the runoff in France's two-round system.

The French state that existed in 2002 was not the French state which exists today. Nearly every losing party endorsed Chirac, giving him more than 82% of the vote. This set the mold for a fashionable myth: that the respectable right wing would never vote for the extreme right, that mainstream conservatism knew its limits and would never exceed them. This let the "patriotic camp" do two things. It could claim that it was the only true threat to the state, and it could claim that the Right of Jacques Chirac was a hollow facsimile of true conservatism. They've maintained this critique up to today. Long perfected by the National Rally and its allies, it's now been turned on them by Zemmour and Reconquête.

That's because the way that the National Front made its route towards political power and mainstream respectability was through a media heavy strategy of "*dediabolisation*," which can be loosely translated as "un-deviling." The media were Le Pen's eager hand maidens in banalizing just how reactionary her beliefs are.

This strategy disillusioned voters. In Hauts-de-France, a region framed at 90 degrees by Belgium to the East and the English Channel to the North, the party was smashed in the 2021 regional election. In one village, Montdidier, their vote tumbled from 43 percent to 22 percent. The reason, a business owner named Lionel Swaenepoel told *Politico*,[62] was that "people are fed up."

"Marine Le Pen isn't aggressive enough, unlike her father. We don't give a fig about her party manifesto, about her economic program, we want her to kick the migrants out."

Jean-Pascal Devaux, a retired electrician who also talked with *Politico* echoed this.

"She is moving away from the fundamental values of the party," he said. "When I listen to her, she sounds almost left-wing and she's far too soft on crime and immigration."

It caused splits in the party too. The hardline conservative wing of the party in the South-East of the country, represented by Marine Le Pen's niece Marion Maréchal detested this transformation. It explains in no small part why Maréchal endorsed Zemmour and betrayed her aunt.

In Mid-October 2021, Marine le Pen was riding high in the polls at around 26%. Neck and neck with Macron, it seemed unlikely that there could be any other candidate facing Macron in the second round of the French presidential election.

Since then, Zemmour has cut into her numbers. He reached as high as 16% – enough to make it into the runoff. But since then he's declined to around 4th or 5th place, dipping under and above the 10% mark. This drop in the polls is likely a combination of the war in Ukraine making him a target for attacks that he supported the Russian President Vladimir Putin, and voters in the patriotic camp rallying around Le Pen as the most likely candidate to make the runoff against Macron. It also has opened space for the social democratic candidate Jean-Luc Mélenchon, running for the third time in 2022, to possibly make the runoff – ahead of the first round of the election on April 10th, 2022, he has maintained a rising position at 3rd place, just below Marine Le Pen.

In *France Hasn't Said Its Last Word*, Zemmour tells a story about meeting with Le Pen in 2021. "I know what you want to do," Le Pen told Zemmour. "Present yourself for the LR primary to become their candidate, but they won't let you do it. There's too much money at play."

Zemmour replied, smiling, that this wasn't his intention, despite what several of his friends were advising him to do. Le Pen seemed shocked by that. She was sure of her information.

A few days before their meeting, Zemmour recounted, there'd been a poll showing her at 48% of voting intentions against Macron in the second round. "This flattering figure had produced a joy that lit up her face," wrote Zemmour. But he reminded her that during each presidential election, the polls a year out from the election were never born out.

"In 2016, Juppe was predicted to be the winner; in 2011, Strauss-Kahn; in 2001, Jospin; in 1994, Balladur. And I could go back like this all the way up to de Gaulle!"

Le Pen warned Zemmour that politics was miserable, and that he wouldn't get more than 3% of the vote. Worse, even, all he'll accomplish was to stop her from winning. Zemmour countered this by saying that *he* thought it was Macron who wanted her in the second round so that he could easily win.

"'The system' [was] interested in her being in the second round," he told her.

"The system doesn't exist," she replied. "She believed in the polls," explained Zemmour.

That encounter happened before Zemmour announced he was running. At one point, it looked like this schism in the patriotic camp could open up the presidential race to another candidate of the Right, Valérie Pécresse. Pécresse had been Nicolas Sarkozy's Budget minister, and many pundits thought she could beat Macron.

Julie Apricena, an official in the National Rally's youth wing, said in February that she was convinced Zemmour had been planted in the race to help Valérie Pécresse. "That's a shared opinion," she insisted, not just something she believes. "[D]uring our meetings and also in our trips on the ground lots of people are already scared of Éric Zemmour."[63]

Les Républicains was a rebrand of UMP, Sarkozy's political party (LR also allowed Sarkozy to exercise much more personal power over a party that had predated him, remaking it in his own image). But Pécresse, allegedly a safe alternative to the extreme fringe which Zemmour represents, often sounds no different from him.

"Emmanuel Macron's new challenger from the center-right must resist the 'Zemmourisation' of her party," wrote the *Guardian*'s editorial board in December 2021 in an article titled "The Guardian view on French Gaullists: keeping the far right at bay."[64]

But this time around, Pécresse could never be a "soft" "business conservative," even if she wanted to or if such a thing existed. Second place in the LR primary went to Éric Ciotti, who even the *Guardian* reported was "promised a central role in her campaign."[65]

During the primary Ciotti trailed Marine Le Pen closely, proposing a referendum on mass immigration which had long been the promise of the National Rally candidate if she won. France, for Ciotti too, must remain French. And the war on terror in France should be expanded and deepened, with a "French Guantanamo Bay" opened up under him.

Ciotti won around 25% of the vote in the first round of the primary, first place among the challengers. Later, he promised that if the election came to a run-off between Emmanuel Macron and Éric Zemmour, he would vote for Zemmour. The reason, he said, was that Zemmour shared his analysis of the state of the country.

He performed worse in the second-round runoff, getting just under 40 percent of the vote; his influence, however, on Pécresse's campaign was powerful. Pécresse, already running to the right during the primary campaign, went further in February, using the phrase "the Great Replacement" to the outrage of the media class who had elevated and nourished Zemmout at every turn.

"I understand the anger of a people who feel powerless against violence, Islamist separatism and uncontrolled immigration," Pécresse said afer winning the primary. "I will not have a wavering hand against the enemies of the Republic."

Pécresse has fallen in the polls too – two weeks out from the first round vote on April 10th, she hovered around 10%. But she was just another example of how Zemmour's ideas were on the march.

In her meeting with Zemmour, Le Pen confessed that after the 2017 presidential debate she didn't think she'd be able to go on. She had been roundly derided then for an amateur performance.

"I really wanted to stop everything," Le Pen told Zemmour, "you didn't spare me…"

Here, he had to interrupt her.

"Pardon, but you were lamentable. You humiliated all of us. Since we're in the same [political] family, if my sister was doing nonsense, I [would] tell her."

Le Pen tried to push back, but Zemmour was firm.

"Frankly, I don't believe that you're going to win. I also think that you're the only chance Macron has to win. Voting for you, is voting for Macron. In any case, he knows it and will do anything to make you go up."

A Pack of Hypocrites

One of Zemmour's most fundamental complaints about the French right is that he believes they try far too much to appeal to the left. Worse, *it wants* the approval of the left. This was Nicolas Sarkozy's fatal mistake when he lost his reelection campaign in 2012, says Zemmour: he wasn't right wing enough. For instance, he would not take his adviser Patrick Buisson,'s advice on holding a referendum on immigration. This referendum has long been a plank of the National Rally's program. Like Zemmour, they say immigration was imposed from above on the French people by politicians who never asked them what they wanted. Ask the French people what they want, their theory goes, and they will reject it.

Where Zemmour differs from the National Rally is in the explicitly right-wing character of this pitch. The National Rally sees the entire Vth Republic tainted by the soft hand of the left and the right, working in lockstep together to enact an agenda against the sovereign French people. This seems very similar to Zemmour, but there is a difference. De Gaulle is Zemmour's lodestar, and, though he agrees with this general analysis, he doesn't reject the right. Instead, he says the right in government has gone soft in their attempt to appeal to the left. Zemmour himself is unabashed about him being a man of the right – the true right.

He devotes a few pages in *France Hasn't Said Its Last Word* to write about the National Museum of Immigration – a metaphor for the policy of multiculturalism, he says, and poorly attended. The museum is "a co-production of the right and the left. An idea of the left put in place by the right." The idea was launched by the Socialist Prime Minister Lionel Jospin, Zemmour writes, then put in place by Jacques Chirac after he added it to his electoral program. The idea was first proposed by a historian of immigration, Gérard Noiriel, an "old Marxist militant recycled by the university networks by the Godfather of sociology, Pierre Bourdieu, who swapped the defense of workers for the defense of immigrants."

The poor attendance at the museum had a simple reason, Zemmour proposed, which those who govern France couldn't understand. While they believe that the French people simply didn't understand the message of the museum and their reticence to visit was the simple result of a "communication deficit," Zemmour says the reason is just the opposite.

"The French people understand well; and maybe too well. They grasped strongly that the museum would be dedicated to the glory of African and Maghrebi immigrants." Not only would it glorify them, but it would glorify them in an attempt to "denounce" and "overwhelm" France.

The right is like this, explains Zemmour, because they are never really true to their convictions. And Zemmour knows this because he knows the political class. Despite his pretensions to the contrary, he has enjoyed deep access to the French political class over the past two decades from his perch as a columnist at *Le Figaro*, the mainstream French conservative newspaper. *France Hasn't Said Its Last Word* is littered with stories that make this point. Zemmour dines with Chirac, Zemmour dines with Sarkozy, Zemmour keeps the sexual secrets of these men because he finds that reporting on them is "an odious American habit."

Take Sarkozy. Zemmour knows that Sarkozy isn't really as right wing as he says he is. Zemmour uses the example of Jean-François Copé, a spokesman for Sarkozy's government. He tells Zemmour that he supports gay marriage. The reason he supports this, reveals Zemmour with a flourish, is that two of Copé's counselors are gay and live together. But afterwards, Zemmour sees Copé at the anti-gay marriage *Manif pour tous*.

This kind of story is common in the book. Zemmour reveals a prominent figure who he's personally friendly with and is right wing in public but left wing in private, or left wing in public and right wing in private. The entire political class then is a pack of hypocrites. Only Zemmour stands above the fray, ready to replace it.

The Great Replacement

For Éric Zemmour, you can see the reality of the Great Replacement even in French cinema. "Already, the France that we knew in the 1960s has disappeared," he writes in *France Hasn't Said Its Last Word*. "It suffices to watch the films from this era to perceive it. The 'Great Replacement' is neither a myth, nor a conspiracy, but a relentless process." "This identitarian question," he continues,

> "renders all others subaltern, even the most important like school, industry, social protection, the place of France in the world. I am certain that not a single candidate – even Marine Le Pen – will dare to impose this identitarian and civilizational struggle at the heart of the campaign. We'll speak of security, of souverainity, independence, of offshoring. Marine Le Pen already talks like Emmanuel Macron who talks like Marine Le Pen. Only Jean-Luc Mélenchon dares to evoke the subject, but to glorify the future of a mixed France, 'créolisée,' his new fetish word, borrowed from the poet Glissant (and even though the Creoles were originally whites of the American islands colonized by France). A 'créolisation,' a mixing, is nothing but the *cache-sexe* of a much more simple operation, 'Islamization': The inexorable introduction of France, ancient Christian land for two thousand years, into the general Islamic Ummah."[66]

There's an especially venomous chapter where Zemmour talks about a 2006 movie called *Indigènes*. Zemmour gnashes his teeth describing the "false" ideology he says the movie promotes. The film, directed by Rachid Bouchareb, purports to tell the story of Maghrebis in the French colonial army and their role both fighting in the Second World War, then rebuilding the country afterwards.

Zemmour quotes Bouchareb condescendingly, calling

Bouchareb's gusto a pleasure to watch. "It was us who liberated Marseille," gushed Bouchareb, "Toulon, Monte Cassino, Corsica... we took the first bullets, it was us who were on the front line."

Zemmour derogatively calls this the *Iliad* and the *Odyssey*: fantasies, an attempt at new founding myths for France. "The fathers and the grandparents of the 'children of immigration' were heroes who liberated France at the end of their guns; and right after they threw their guns down, they picked up their trowels and rebuilt the country; they weren't men anymore, but demi-gods," he sneers.

Zemmour has a litany of complaints about this narrative, whipping himself up into a frenzy as he denounces it. The narrative, says Zemmour, is "historically false but politically correct." He says the narrative is a colonizing narrative, not an assimilationist one, an attempt to install a new aristocracy of immigrants over the native population of France, like the Franks over the Gauls after the fall of Rome.

Bouchareb has "the attitude of a colonizer, not an immigrant." Worse for Zemmour, he doesn't respect the modern history of France, but tries to replace it.

In another section of the book, Zemmour defends Maurice Papon. Attempts to blacken his name, writes Zemmour, are the same sorts of attacks on history as a movie like *Indigènes*.

Papon was a police prefect who facilitated the deportation of French Jews during the Nazi occupation. Under Papon, 1,560 Parisian Jews were deported to concentration camps. He was also responsible for a notorious massacre in Paris in 1961. On October 17th of that year, the Paris police were ordered by Papon to move against protestors from the Algerian National Liberation Front who were protesting France's actions in the war. They were breaking a curfew Papon had handed down, so he used this as a pretext to order his police forces to take deadly action. They killed hundreds the night of the 17th; on a bridge near Saint Michel, police shot protestors and pushed them into the Seine river. That same year, de Gaulle personally gave Papon the *Ordre national de la Légion d'honneur*, France's highest civilian and military honor.

Zemmour adduces de Gaulle's approval of Papon's defense of Vichy France to counter charges that it was a criminal regime. If de Gaulle approved of people like Papon, and even appointed former Vichy officials into his governments, then how could Vichy have been criminal? If Vichy was criminal, Zemmour asks, wouldn't that make de Gaulle criminal too?

It's this aspect of the Gaullist personality cult which dominates French politics that gives it such potency in laundering reactionary and fascist ideas into the mainstream. When French audiences read Zemmour's challenge, they're supposed to find the idea that de Gaulle could be a criminal absurd. Even the implication that de Gaulle is a criminal is an unsupportable premise. It's in exactly this way that Zemmour uses the power and attraction of de Gaulle's personality cult to justify his reactionary cant: it's not me saying this after all, he seems to smirk, it's *de Gaulle*. And, of course, he isn't wrong. That *was* de Gaulle.

If we approach this without the premise that de Gaulle is sacrosanct, then the idea that Vichy was a criminal regime because it deported French Jews to concentration camps isn't absurd. And it's only a small leap from there that a man who honored an official of this regime who was responsible for these deportations, as well as massacres under his own government, with the Legion of Honor, might be a criminal himself.

But in Zemmour's cosmogony, de Gaulle cannot be a criminal. This is part of the patriotic mythology that forms the fabric of the Vth Republic, and a box from which anguished French patriots cannot escape. To criticize Zemmour genuinely they have to admit criticism of the patron saint of the Republic, Charles de Gaulle.

Listen to Zemmour, however, and national mythology is being replaced because of the demographic pressure on the country. The cult of personality of de Gaulle is dying, Zemmour believes, because the reality of the French nation is dying. But France, says Zemmour, is not just an idea, but a nation composed of people, with two thousand years of history. If he can preserve these people through a demographic offensive, then he can save those ideas so dear to him and the aristocratic, bourgeois world he adopted. These ideas, in the world that Zemmour grew up in, were not controversial.

"I defended the country, order, merit, hierarchy, excellence, assimilation. My discourse would have been banal in the 60s; after the great shakeup of the 70s, it was revolutionary. Revolutionary because it was reactionary."

It's this sort of pseudo-taboo-breaking – by defending all the taboos which 1968 broke – that helps explain the appeal of Zemmour's ideas, which shows no sign of waning. Many on the right think that, no matter what happens in the 2022 election, Zemmour will run again in 2027. Zemmour constantly reminds his crowd that he's not a professional politician, but everything indicates now that he's launching a career as one. With even just 10% of the vote, he can justify remaining a presence in French political life. That was Jean-Marie Le Pen's score in 2007, after all. The elder Le Pen, who launched French reaction's post-war offensive, dined with Zemmour in January 2020. Along with his wife Jainy, Le Pen brought Ursula Painvin. She is the daughter of Joachim von Ribbentrop, Hitler's Foreign Minister.

"It's hard to call [Zemmour] a Nazi or a fascist," Jean-Marie crowed in an interview with *Le Monde*. This gives him greater freedom."

"The only difference between Éric and me," he went on, "is that he's Jewish."

Endnotes

1   «Je suis assimilé, arabe à l'extérieur, français à l'intérieur».
Dominique Albertini, "Jean Messiha, un cadre atypique au FN,"
Libération, February 10, 2017.

2   Marie-Pierre Bourgeois, "Présidentielle: Comment Zemmour
se sert de la Seine-Saint-Denis pour son discours politique," BF-
MTV, February 9, 2022.

3   Christophe Forcari, "Portrait: Popu mais content," Libéra-
tion, July 5, 2006.

4   Éric Zemmour, "28 Jan 2022," interview by Cyril Hanouna,
Face à Baba, C8, January 28, 2022, video.

5   Éric Zemmour, interview by Patrick Cohen, C à vous, France
Télévisions, February 16, 2022, video.

6   "Présidentielle: Éric Zemmour bénit la colonisation
Française," BFM avec RMC, March 21, 2022.

7   Vincent Trémolet de Villers, "Immigration: l'incroyable aveu
de François Hollande," Le Figaro, October 12, 2016.

8   "Immigration, "grand remplacement": Macron reprend en
privé des formules d'Éric Zemmour et Renaud Camus," Valeurs
Actuelles, November 24, 2020.

9   Macron, Emmanuel, "La lettre aux Français d'Emmanuel Macron, dans lequel il annonce sa candidature," March 3, 2022.

10   Christophe Lefèvre, Interview with the author, February 17th, 2022.

11   Éric Zemmour, "Le Grand Rendez-vous du 26/09/2021" hosted by by Sonia Mabrouk, Le Grand Rendez-vous, C News, September 26, 2022.

12   As for Zemmour's personal faith, he says he is not a believer.

13   "I think there's a problem with the Chechen community in France," Mélenchon said after a teacher was beheaded by a young Chechen in Yvelines in 2020. See "Attentat de Conflans: Jean-Luc Mélenchon estime qu'il y a «un problème avec la communauté tchétchène»," 20minutes, October 18, 2020.

14   "Qu'est-ce que la créolisation? Entretien avec Jean-Luc Mélenchon," l'Insoumission, September 4, 2021.

15   Julian Jackson, A Certain Idea of France: The Life of Charles de Gaulle (Allen Lane, 2018), 197.

16   Jacques Fauvet, La IVe république (Paris: Librairie Arthème Fayard, 1959), 35.

17   His association with the party, however, hardly lasted a week; he found its fascist character too transparent.

18   Marie-Claire Lavabre and François Platone, Que reste-t-il du PCF? (Paris: Autrement / CÉVIPOF (Centre d'études de la vie politique française), 2003), 6.

19   Fauvet, 33.

20   Bizerte, in fact, was the last city which the French managed

to hold onto in Algeria after the rest of the country had already become independent.

21   Influence because, while the Northern part of the country was directly occupied by the Nazis, the Southern half of the country, known as Vichy France, remained, however nominally, and independent French state. De Gaulle tried to avoid attacking Vichy forces directly – he considered the loss of French lives intolerable – and trained his forces on the German occupiers.

22   Hélène Carrère d'Encausse, Le Général De Gaulle et la Russie (Fayard, 2017), 42.

23   La Cagoule was a shadowy anti-communist terrorist organization founded in 1935 to overthrow the Popular Front government. A "cagoule" is a cowl, a nickname they were given by the fascist press. Its members were initiated into the organization through cultish rituals involving torches and swords, with the initiators dressed all in black and the grand master garbed in Red. Initiates would recite a Latin oath which meant "For the greater glory of France." The group received funding from reactionary French industrialists like Eugène Schueller, who founded the L'Oréal cosmetics corporation. They carried out a series of bombings and assassinations, among other violent acts, some of which were designed to be blamed on Communists.

24   Quoted in Jackson, 529.

25   Fauvet, 33-34.

26   Marine Le Pen's "National Front" party, of course, was named in an ironic nod to the resistance organization. And today, there is a magazine called *Le Franc-Tireur* – its star essayist is the particularly execrable Raphaël Enthoven, a pseudo-intellec-

tual, West Parisian "philosopher" from a rich family (he became famous in France for once dating the pop musician Carla Bruni, appearing on the cover of the popular magazine Paris-Match with her; she later married President Nicolas Sarkozy). In June 2021 he said that, faced with the choice between the social democratic candidate Jean-Luc Mélenchon and the fascist Marine Le Pen, he would choose Le Pen. "Rather [Donald] Trump than [Hugo] Chavez," he explained: "...j'irais à 19h59 voter pour Marine Le Pen en me disant, sans y croire, « Plutôt Trump que Chavez. »" (@Enthoven_R, June 7, 2021).

Covers of *Le Franc-Tireur* feature headlines like "Europe, sponsor of Islamists," warning about tens of millions of dollars of subsidies given to the Muslim Brotherhood, and "Schools, a warning against separatism," where a cartoon shows a man with a large bushy beard wearing a taqiyah (the traditional skullcap some Muslim men wear) gleefully pouring a bucket of sewage into a student with a lobotomized expression's head. In the March 23rd, 2022, issue (the latest issue as of this writing), a cartoon of an unshaven Jean-Luc Mélenchon appears on the cover under the headline "The betrayals of Mélenchon." The social democratic politician is accused of supporting "Islamo-Gauchistes," or Islamo-leftists, a crude present-day reinvention of the Judeo-Bolshevik myth.

These are just two examples of how French reaction is particularly willing to appropriate the language and iconography of the Resistance and fashion them towards their own ends.

27   Fauvet, 34.

28   Quoted in Fauvet, 34n1.

29   Fauvet, 56.

30 Lavabre and Platone, 22.

31 Ibid.

32 Lavabre and Platone, 29-30.

33 Samuel Laurent et Leila Marchand, "Le FN dit-il la même chose que les communistes il y a trente ans ?" Le Monde, April 20, 2015.

34 Georgs Marchais, "Georges Marchais répond au recteur de la mosquée de Paris," L'Humanité, June 7, 1981, availble at http://uncoupdevent.blogspot.com/2011/06/la-vraie-lettre-de-georges-marchais-au.html.

35 Marie-Pierre Bourgeois, "'Il parlait exactement comme moi': Éric Zemmour se compare à Georges Marchais sur l'immigration," BFMTV, February 9th, 2022.

36 Lavabre and Platone, 30-31.

37 Ibid.

38 Ibid, 36.

39 Ibid, 48.

40 Fabien Roussel, "Disparition de Jacques Chirac," Parti communiste français, September 26, 2019.

41 Ian H. Birchall, "Gaullism in Retrospect," International Socialism no. 58 (May 1973): 17-18.

42 A Bonapartist order is one where a powerful and popular military leader leads a firm rule based on the legitimacy of alleged mass popular support.

43 Jonathan Fenby, The General Charles De Gaulle and the

France He Saved (London: Simon & Schuster, 2010), 413.

44   Ibid, 412.

45   And tests in Algeria continued until 1966 – a secret protocol in the Évian Accords which recognized Algeria's independence allowed the testing to continue.

46   The 18th brumaire was November 9, 1799, on the French revolutionary character. It was the day Napoleon first declared himself Emperor. The next day, the general Joachim Murat, known as "Napoleon's sword," marched a troop of grenadiers into the Council of Five Hundred, the legislature of the French revolutionary constitution. "Citizens!" he shouted. "You are dissolved." The deputies fled out of any exit they could find, including the windows. Éric Zemmour, Le Suicide français (Albin Michel, 2014).

47   Jackson, xxxi.

48   A long, loose-fitting robe worn in North Africa.

49   Quoted in Jackson, 511.

50   De Gaulle's exact phrase was "Voulez-vous être bougnoulisés," a transformation of the noun "bougnole" into a crude verb. "Bougnoule" is a particularly offensive ethnic slur aimed specifically at North Africans. It can be translated variously as "raghead," "towelhead," "camel-fucker," or "n****r." I've translated it thus here to capture the true nastiness of the word in English. Quoted in Jackson, 854n12.

51   Jackson, 512.

52   Modern day Burkina Faso.

53   Dirty Work 2: The CIA in Africa, ed. Ellen Ray, William Schaap, et. al. (Lyle Stuart, 1979), 25.

54   Éric Zemmour, Un quinquennat pour rien (Paris: Éditions Albin Michel, 2016), 309.

55   Fauvet, 9-10.

56   Fauvet, 10-11.

57   "Lettre Ouvert A Nos Gouvernants," Place d'Armes, April 14, 2021.

58   Suburbs, in French.

59   "The Hexagone" is a figure of speech referring to the roughly hexagonal shape of mainland France.

60   Colbertism is an economic philosophy that holds that the state has primacy over the economy, and the economy should be tailored to furthering the greatness of the state and the nation. It was particularly preoccupied with accumulating precious metals like gold. Its name comes from Jean-Baptiste Colbert, Louis XIV's Controller-General of Finances.

61   Interview with the author, February 2022.

62   Clea Caulcutt, "Xavier Bertrand, the ex-insurance salesman who 'smashed the jaws' of the French far-right," Politico, June 25, 2021.

63   Interview with the author, February 2022.

64   "The Guardian view on French Gaullists: keeping the far right at bay," The Guardian, December 12, 2021.

65   Angelique Chrisafis, "Hard-right French MP tops Les Ré-

publicains party's presidential primary," The Guardian, December 2, 2021.

66   Ummah, Arabic for 'community,' refers to the collective global Islamic community.

Lightning Source UK Ltd.
Milton Keynes UK
UKHW011847060422
401188UK00001B/4